The Time Came

Donald A. Peart

The Time Came Copyright © 2007 Donald A. Peart

ISBN: 978-0-9886897-8-7

Edition: September 2022

REFERENCES

All scriptures are quoted from the King James Version, unless otherwise noted.

All <u>underscoring</u>, parenthetical notes, brackets, bold lettering, literal definitions of the Scriptures in this text are supplied by the author. They are supplied for emphasis and clarity. All single quotes within the Scriptures are the literal Greek definitions inserted by the author for clarity. Words such as "thee," "thine," "ye," "thou" and words ending in "th," and so on are replaced with the appropriate modern renditions for easy reading.

Strong's Exhaustive Concordance
Vines Expository Dictionary
Thayer's Lexicon
Bible Works Software
BibleSoft Software

TABLE OF CONTENTS

ACKNOWLEDGMENTS

"For it seemed good to the Holy Spirit" (Acts 15:28a) with whom I deliberated much, telling Him why I was concerned, as Paul did in Galatians 2:2. Nevertheless, I was obedient to the Holy Spirit. I did not want to hide this "talent" in my "earth."

COMMENTS

My expectation after completing this book is that this book would provide an understandable "pattern" of the signs of the times in order for readers to continue to prepare, or begin the preparation by adjusting their lives, for the eventuality to "meet" our King—Jesus—without fear. Preparation usually provides the best advantage for an opportunity. Understanding what the Church ought to do relative to "time" should give those who obtain it the advantage of "internal preparation" "against that day." We adjust our lives now because Jesus' appearing (lit., "epiphany") is sure to come.

The Lord directed Ezekiel to show the "pattern"[1] of the "house to the house of Israel." The Lord also stated that if the house of Israel were "ashamed" of their "wrong," after they saw Jesus' "pattern," then they would be shown the "adjustments." God is "not willing that any should perish." He desires that all His people adjust their lives now, as we patiently wait for His promised coming. Saying it another way: Jesus wants us to be just like Him when He appears; and those who have this "expectation" in them purify themselves as Jesus is pure.

Finally, I understand that "the dominion" of "the enactments of heaven" is also put in the earth through writing (Job 38:33). Thus, Jesus sends scribes to teach by writing the "times" concerning "the enactments" of His dominion (kingdom) which is filling the habitable world and the earth (Luke 11:49, Matthew 23:34, Revelation 1:11, Ecclesiastes 12:12b). Thus, I also recommend that some of my other titles (electronic or paper) be referenced with this book: "The Numbers of God" and "The Completions of the Ages (The Gate, the Door and the Veil)." "Daniel understood by books the number of the years ... unto the Messiah the Prince ..." (Daniel 9:2 w/Daniel 9:25).

---

[1] Hebrew "thknith" (תבנית), which can yield the Hebrew pictograph of "my-so" (כני) between the two crosses (ת) or crucified ones. Jesus, God's "so" between the two crucified ones on His left and right; "so" being defined as the manner as intended. That is, Jesus crucified between the two thieves is the manner God intended relative to God's eternal purposes.

May you understand the writing of the Scriptures concerning the "set times" of Jesus, who shall show in His appearing (lit., epiphany) that He is the only Potentate, the King of kings, and the Lord of lords (see 1 Timothy 6:14-16).

PREFACE

Jesus is to return in the same way He was taken into heaven. Yet, there appears to be a lull for some in the Church and in the world concerning the coming of our Lord Jesus and the promised 1,000 years rule of "the Christ" and His saints "<u>with</u>" Him. The world is saying the predictors of Jesus' coming have "cried wolf" too many times and nothing has happened. Some have forgotten the "pattern" of events that Paul said must occur "first," as outlined in 2 Thessalonians 2:1-3.

The book of Daniel also foretold events that must occur. Another understanding is that the "pattern" set forth by Jesus must also be fulfilled. That is, the end may not come until the gospel of the kingdom is preached in all the occupied houses as a witness unto all nations (Matthew 24:14). Some have not known these patterns and other patterns and have made unbiblical predictions.

Thus, the already doubting world is questioning the truth of the coming of the Lord Jesus; and they are becoming more cynical. The mockers in the Church are also questioning Jesus' promised coming. This is seen by the way they live their lives. They are asking "where is the promise of His coming?" Well, according to Daniel, "the Ancient of Days came ... and the time came" (Daniel 7:22).

Just as God "timed" Jesus' first coming (Matthew 2:7), so the promise of His returning the same way He left, is "timed" (Luke 12:45; 2 Peter 3:4, 7); and, according to Daniel, "the Ancient of Days (Jesus) came ... and the time came." Even though the Lord has "timed" His coming, it does not mean that He will never come (Luke 12:45, see Greek word for "delay").

"The day of the Lord will come..." (2 Peter 3:10). "He that shall come will come..." (Hebrews 10:37). It is an historical truth that Jesus came approximately 2,000 years ago. It will also be an historical truth that Jesus, "the Ancient of Days" — will come again. It is all in His timing! "The saints will possess the kingdom;" because "the time came." The

iv

time of this present evil age will end or be completed as we know it; and the seventh trumpet is sounding with a "clear" sound to prepare the saints for their time, <u>both now and future.</u>

As surely as John prepared the saints for the "last time" (lit., "hour") in his days by showing them the pattern of the last hour (1 John 2:18), there is also written in the Bible a surer prophetic word or prophetic pattern for the last hour for this present evil age (2 Peter 1:19). Jesus has said: "The time is fulfilled, and the kingdom of God is at hand: repent you and believe the gospel" (Mark 1:15).

Looking forward to the chapters that follow, I believe that this book will encourage you to mindfully wait for the coming of the Lord Jesus through an understanding of the times and seasons. I pray also that this book may aid in building up your most holy faith in Jesus by the power of the Holy Spirit that you may become the same stature as Jesus.

May the love of our Lord Jesus Christ which is poured into us by the Holy Spirit continue to strengthen the hearts of all the saints that "when He shall appear, we may have confidence, and not be ashamed before Him at His coming" (1 John 2:28). Jesus is King, now! Jesus is Lord, now!

JESUS, THE END

Jesus is called "the first and the last." We generally look at time as linear. However, what about circular time? Time "began" with Jesus; it will "end" through Jesus. Make sure He is in you; and that you are "into" Him. Jesus is the "Beginning."

Colossians 1:18: and he is the head of the body, the church: who is the **beginning**....

Genesis 1:1: **In the beginning** *God created the heaven and the earth.*

According, to Genesis 1:1, God created "in the beginning." That is, God created "in" Jesus **"who is the beginning."** Jesus was the One who "travailed in birth pain"[2] to create the "ages" as we know them and the age to come as some will know it. Jesus is also related to the end of these times as we know them. Jesus is the "end."

Hebrews 1:2: Hath in these last days spoken unto us by His Son, whom He hath appointed heir of all things, by whom also **He made the worlds (lit., ages)**

Revelation 21:6: and He said unto me, it is done. **I am** *Alpha and Omega, the* **beginning, and the end.**

Thus, the end is also "in" Him. Whatever our opinion is of time, when time is up as we know it, Jesus will be there in the "last." In fact, remember that Jesus stated that He is "the end...and the last."

Revelation 22:13: I am Alpha and Omega, **the beginning,** *and* **the end, the first** *and* **the last.**

Since Jesus is "the end" and "the last," I must say that any inquiry into time will be an unsuccessful search without a genuine relationship with the Son of God, who is Jesus, the Christ. There is a real, living "flesh and bone" Jesus in heaven and His Holy Spirit is

---

[2] Proverbs 8 with 1 Corinthians 1:30 with Hebrews 1:2

1

also in us! He is not dead! He is living! Genuine relationship with Jesus is paramount.

Some are so enamored with the end of time (eschatology) that they have not considered Jesus, who is their beginning and who is also their end. Some have not considered that without genuine relationship with Jesus, the end of living life is "crisis" in death. Remember, that man is appointed to die once; and after a person dies, the "crisis" of God's judgment becomes a reality (Hebrews 9:27).

They do not know the **"Person"** of Life in their **"deep thoughts"** (Hebrews 1:1-3; 1 John 5:20). They do not understand that without Jesus there is no extension in the opportunities of the Kingdom of God beyond their physical death. And when the end of the ends does come, they will have no apparent end in the second death. Now that's torment! We need Jesus, His blood, His Word, His Spirit, and His Church. Jesus is Savior of our spirit, soul, and body. Jesus is Lord! Jesus is King, now!

With the understanding that Jesus is the end, I want to encourage the readers, again, not to partake of this book looking for superficial security in "calculated time." We are only secure in Jesus. Remember, God's sovereignty and His people are "variables" of time.

Thus, be careful about "calculating" events that can only be brought about by God, through Jesus. Jesus is still Lord. He is still the Lord of the harvest who is waiting patiently for the precious fruits (the early and latter) of the earth (James 5:7, Luke 10:2, Revelation 14).

The Lord can choose to delay His return as long as He wills. If He chooses to delay His coming longer than some may envision, will that cause a person to stop walking with Jesus? Again, one should be careful not to put the autonomy of God on man's timetables.

Yet, we should not walk about aimlessly without any spiritual understanding of the times. "Time" is indeed a very controversial issue in the Church; yet timing is important to God. Jesus was sent forth, birthed from a woman "when the fullness of time was come" (Galatians 4:4).

Humanity in general is also so very time conscious that they spend money on foretelling. Some in the Church will devote hours and spend thousands just to hear a prophecy about their future (If only they could see that the Prophet, Jesus, is <u>also</u> speaking in them?). However, is this pursuit of understanding the times a legitimate pursuit for Jesus' followers and/or humanity in general? It appears to be! Prophets and apostles alike have also cried, "How long Lord?"

One of the keys is "who" are Jesus' followers and humanity in general seeking for the understanding of the times? Are they seeking the only true heavenly Father and His Word through His "Clean Spirit?" Or are they seeking men or women who speak from themselves and/or are they seeking words from "unclean spirits?" There are many who claim to have the answer of timing; but there is only one Jesus who can give "the answer" concerning the remaining "years" that will bring an **"answer of peace"** to the inquirers (Genesis 41:16; 26; 27).

"The seven years of plenteousness" rule for the world's kingdoms will "end;" and the answer of Jesus is the only **"answer of peace"** that will satisfy the hearts of all mankind in regard to "the end." There are also those who, like Jesus, do indeed speak from God, with God's words; and they have part of the "answer of peace" for His people and any from the world who may inquire of the Lord Jesus. Leaders, especially apostles and prophets should "know" the signs of the times; and they should have competent answers for God's people. Jesus does indeed expect those who have "understanding of the times to know what Israel (the Church of Jesus) ought to do" (1 Chronicles 12:32 w/John 3:10).

*1 Chronicles 12:32: And of the children of **Issachar**, which were men that had **understanding of the times**, to know what Israel ought to do....*

*John 3:10: Jesus answered and said unto him, Art you a master of Israel, and **know not these things?***

He also expects those who know times to be able to impart this "understanding of times" through the Spirit of Truth to His followers (Matthew 26:18; 2 Thessalonians 2:5-6). Jesus also expects the Daniels and Josephs of these days to explain the set times of Jesus as to when "the seven years of plenteousness" will "end;" and that in the days of the voice of the seventh (last) trumpet, the kingdoms of this world will be translated to the Kingdom of the Lord and His Christ (see Genesis 41; Daniel 2; Daniel 5; Revelation 10, Revelation 11, Hebrews 12, and so on).

The statement above may seem to place demand on leaders to have answers. However, Jesus really does expect some to discern the times. In the same way mankind has perfected foretelling the weather, Jesus expects His leaders to "discern the signs of the times" through the Spirit of Jesus. Jesus reprimanded the Pharisees for not having the ability to "discern the signs of the times," yet they could predict the weather.

Matthews 16:1-3: [1]The Pharisees also with the Sadducees came and tempting desired him that he would show them a sign from heaven. [2]He answered and said unto them, when it is evening, you say, it will be fair weather: for the sky is red. [3]And in the morning, it will be foul weather today: for the sky is red and lowering. **O you hypocrites, you can discern the face of the sky; but can you not discern the signs of the times?**

The Pharisees perfected predicting the daily weather. Yet, they could not tell what time it was relative to Jesus. Jesus was the end of their self-righteous rule, yet they could not see their end. The Pharisees were blinded from understanding the times because they could not accept Jesus as the Messiah and John as a baptizer. That is a core issue. Understanding the signs of the times is accomplished by accepting Jesus as Messiah, Christ, Savior, Baptizer, King, Lord. The world must believe that Jesus is indeed the Christ. It is not necessarily telling the exact year, month, week, day, hour, minute and second that prepares one for the times to come.

Does a person have such a relationship with Jesus that he/she will be able to discern the sign of the seasons (plural) and times (plural), through God's Word, through the supply of the Holy Spirit, and by the teaching of genuine ministers of God?

Or will the Day of the Lord surprise them as those who have no hope in Jesus? Do you know Jesus, or rather are you known by Him (Galatians 4:9)? Has the **"Spirit of Jesus"** taught you how to discern "exactly" the times and seasons relative to **your lifetime** (1 John 2:20)?

The Holy Spirit told Simeon that "he (Simeon) should **not see death,** before he had seen the Lord's Christ" (Luke 2:26). The same words were said about Enoch. Enoch **"did not see death,"** either (Hebrews 11:5). Now note: Enoch lived 365 years before God translated him. Thus, if Simeon had to live to be 365 years, like Enoch, to see Jesus, he would have lived that long.

The **"Clean Spirit"** gave Simeon a revelation about seeing the Lord's Christ that was attained in Simeon's lifetime. The same is true today. God has raised apostles and prophets who will be able to teach His Church "times and seasons" about the Day of the Lord's Christ by His Holy Spirit sent down from heaven, through patterns in the Scriptures.

Note, I did not say they will be predicting the exact time of Jesus' coming. That day is only known to the Lord. I did not say they would be setting exact dates and years. That would be absurd (Matthew 25: 13; Luke 12:40)! Only the Lord knows the exact time (Zechariah 14:7). However, there will be competent ministers (male and female) who will understand patterns of the times (plural) and seasons (plural) and patterns of the "signs of the times" (1 Chronicles 12:32; 1 Thessalonians 5:1-4; 1 John 2; Revelation 22:10).

Jesus' apostles and prophets, through the Word of God with the Spirit of God, will instruct His Church (2 Thessalonians 2:5-6; Ephesians 3:1-11). Through God, they will give an answer of peace to His people.

It will <u>not be done</u> by some wily visions[3] or false dreams which are not according to God's Word (Isaiah 8:20; Jeremiah 23). Know this: Jesus said that "error" is a result of <u>not</u> perceiving the Scriptures and <u>not</u> perceiving the power of God.

Everything **"all about"** Jesus, including His being the last ("eschatos"), is written "in the volume **of** the book" (Hebrews 10:7). How do I know this? The Greek word for "of," highlighted above, is **"peri."** We use this word in words like <u>peri</u>meter. "Peri" is defined as: "all around," all about," "through (all over)." "The volume of the book" is **"all about" Jesus.**

Jesus, Paul, Peter, and others always substantiated spiritual truths about Jesus by citing the Scriptures as the "witness" (Romans 3:21). Thus, everything "all about" Jesus' "end times," as some call it, that He wants His Church to know is witnessed in the Scriptures. The pattern is sure! It is written!

*Mark 12:24: And Jesus answering said unto them, do you not therefore err, because you know **not the Scriptures**…*

*Luke 4:17: …. And when **He [Jesus]** had opened the book, **He** found the place where it was **written***

*John 5:39: Search the Scriptures; for in them you think you have eternal life: and they are **they which testify of Me [Jesus]**.*

*Revelation 19:12-13: [12]… He [Jesus] had a name written, that no man knew, but He Himself. [13]… and **His name** is called **The Word of God**.*

*Hebrews 10:7: Then said I, Lo, I come (in the volume **of** the book it is written **of Me (lit., all about Me, all around Me, all through Me)** to do your will, O God.*

If Jesus has not written it in the Scripture, then we may not need to know it. And, if He speaks about times in your ears, you can confirm

---

[3] This statement does not negate the fact that God does indeed speak through visions and dreams. In fact, some apostles and prophets of the last days are like Joseph and Daniel, in type, as indicated earlier. See also Acts 2:17.

it in His Word. Be careful of seeking for answers outside the Lord and His Christ (compare 1 Samuel 28:1-19); and it is the Holy Spirit that also bears witness (see1 John 5:6). Everything that Jesus wants us to know **"all about"** the **"character** of His Person" and **"all around"** "the end" is written in "The Word of God" — personified (John 1:1; Acts 4;13; Revelation 19:12-13). He is the living Word who became flesh and tabernacled among us (John 1:14, Hebrews 4:12).

The appearing of Jesus, in person, 2,000 years ago was the sign that that age was effectively over. The change of these ages "into the age" to come is also in a Person, "the Lord's Christ," both head and body. Jesus is "the beginning and **the end.**"

THE EVENING TIME

Zechariah 14:1-7: *¹Behold, the day of the LORD cometh, and your spoil shall be divided in the midst of thee … ⁴And his feet shall stand in that day upon the mount of Olives … ⁵… **the LORD my God shall come, and all the saints with thee.** ⁶And it shall come to pass in that day, that the light shall not be clear, nor dark: ⁷But it shall be **one day** which shall be known to the LORD, not day, nor night: but it shall come to pass, that **at evening time** it shall be light.*

Jesus will indeed return in the same manner in which he left (Acts 1:11-12 with Zechariah 14:4-5). In the verse above, the prophet indicated that the **"time" came** when the Lord Jesus will indeed "come, and all the Saints with [Him]." He also stated that "it shall be one day…." This **"one day"** is the beginning of the "Day of the Lord." This "one day" of the Lord is also one (1) thousand years, as we will see later. (2 Peter 3:8). This "day" is only "known to the Lord." It is a unique day. It is neither "day nor night." Why? **"At evening time, it shall be light."** What does all this mean? When is the "evening time?"

As indicated above, this "one day" of Jesus' coming or "that day" of His coming will occur at the "evening time." This is one of the first hints as to the "times and seasons" of Jesus' coming. I believe that He will come literally **"at the evening time;"** and if you can receive it, this "evening time" is also a **pattern** of **"the evening of this age."** **"The evening"** is significant because God's days begin in the evening and end in the morning. He does not reckon days like most in the world (morning to evening). God reckons His days starting in the evening and ending in the morning. Look at the natural Jews. Their Sabbath always begins on Friday evening and ends on Saturday evenings.

*Genesis 1:5, And God called the light Day, and the darkness he called Night. And the **evening and the morning** were the **first day.***

8

*Genesis 1:8, And God called the firmament Heaven. And **the evening and the morning** were the **second day**.*

Genesis gives us an understanding of God's time. God's days begin in the evening and end in the morning; "and the **evening** and the **morning** were the first day." Genesis <u>did not say</u> that the morning and the evening were the first day. God is opposite man. His day begins in the evening. In other words, when we are ready to go to sleep, He is ready to talk. When it appears dark to us, He says it is a new day! It may be evening (dark) in the world; yet it is the beginning of a new day in God. We are in the evening of this age; and though this age may be ending, it is the beginning of another age. What are some of the patterns of the "evening?"

The **"second lamb"** is offered in the **"evening"** (Numbers 28:4). So likewise at the evening of this age there will be significant martyrdom of soul and/or body for those who become like the Lamb of God — Jesus; and/or those who believe that Jesus is the Christ (Revelation 6:9-11; Matthew 16:24; Revelation 20:1-4; Psalms 105:17-22). The Bible says we are **as** sheep for the slaughter (Romans 8:36).

It was also at the **"time of the offering of the evening sacrifice"** that Elijah judged eight hundred and fifty false prophets. Thus, it shall be in the evening of this age. For every eight hundred-fifty (850) pseudo prophets of Baal[4] and/or prophetesses like Jezebel, there will be only two (2) true prophets with the testimony of Jesus and/or two (2) prophetic Churches that belong to Christ *(see I Kings 18:19-40; Revelation 11:1-13; Revelation 2:20)*. It will be at the evening of this age that God will judge the prophets of Baal, the pseudo god of the sun

---

[4]Baal ((pseudo) master, lord, marriage) is also defined by Jesus as "Satan:" Satan is called Beelzebub (master of flies, demons), Baal-peor (master of gap, yawn, open mouth, spiritual and physical fornication, sexual adultery, homosexuality), Baal-hermon (master of seclusion, devoted to religious use, flat nose (no discernment), Baal-hamon (master of the multitude, wealth, noise), Baal-gad (master of luck, fortunate), and Baal-berith (master of covenant (with death)).

(fire) and prophets of Asherah (goddess of happiness, sensual love, and increase).

It was **"about the time of the evening oblation"** that **Gabriel (lit., powerful man of God)"** was sent to Daniel with further instruction for understanding the "times" with respect to the Messiah's coming (Daniel 9:21). Daniel originally understood "times" by Jeremiah's book; and God sent the angel to **expand**[5] the 70 years to 490 years (Daniel 9:1). So likewise in the evening of this age God shall also send **"Gabriel(s)"** (apostolic men of God) to give understanding concerning the "coming of the Lord" and concerning that which shall be "poured upon the desolator."

It was **"at evening"** that **Jesus appeared to the apostles** in His resurrection body of "flesh and bone" (John 20:19-29; w/Luke 24:39). Thus, in the evening of this age, Jesus will appear to the fearful apostles of today to witness to them that He is indeed living. Some of the modern "Thomas" will even get a chance to thrust their hands and fingers in the pierced flesh of Jesus' resurrected body. They may even feel a bone or two of this real and living Jesus, who is our Lord (Luke 24:39). There are "set seasons" (plural) of His "appearing" (1 Timothy 6:14-15). Yes, Jesus will appear again and again unto many of the called to empower them with faith to preach the gospel of the kingdom of God and to be a witness of the resurrection of our Lord and Savior Jesus.

It is at the "evening" that mankind cease from their labor (Psalms 104:23). It follows that at the evening of this age "some" of God's people will enter the Sabbatism by **"ceasing from their own works"** (Hebrews 4:10). First, the "Sabbatism" is the Person of Jesus. When we believe "into" Him we believe into His rest. Secondly, the "Sabbatism' is also the seven thousandth year from the first Adam, the day that God rested until Adam sinned (Genesis 2:1-3). God is still waiting for "some" to enter that "day" (1,000 years) of rest He had

---

[5] See my book *The Last Hour, The First Hour, The Forty-second Generation.*

10

originally prepared for Adam and mankind (Hebrews 4:4-5). We are in the evening of the six thousand years from the first Adam or just at the beginning of the seventh thousand years from the first Adam.

*Hebrews 4:9-11, ⁹There remains therefore a **rest (lit., Sabbatism)** to the people of God. ¹⁰For he that is entered into his rest, he also hath **ceased from his own works,** as God did from his. ¹¹Let us **labor (lit., use speed)** therefore to enter into that rest, lest any man fall after the same example of unbelief.*

These are <u>some</u> of the patterns that took place in the evening time, which provides insight into the evening of this age. Now let us look at some of the other signs of the "evening time" as defined by Zechariah with the understanding that our Father has not left us without a pattern in His Word with respect to His coming.

Remember, He will only appear as a thief to them who have no hope in Jesus. He also told us that we would **"know perfectly"** the "times and seasons" (plural) (1 Thessalonians 5:1-3). Jesus also indicated that we should be able to **discern** the **signs** of the time with respect to His visitation (Matthew 16:3). What are the **"signs** of the time" that hint to us that we are about to experience "the age to come?" Let us hear the words of Zechariah again.

*Zechariah 14:5-7, ⁵... the LORD my God shall come, and all the saints with thee. ⁶And it shall come to pass in **that day,** that **the light shall not be clear, nor dark:** ⁷But it shall be one day which shall be known to the LORD, **not day, nor night:** but it shall come to pass, that at **evening time** it shall be **light.***

These are the signs of the evening time, according to Zechariah. One: **"The light** shall not be **clear."** Two: "The light shall not be … **dark."** Three: "It shall be **one day** … not day, nor night … "at evening time it shall be **light."** Let us look at these one by one.

First: One of the signs of the day of Jesus' coming with His Saints in the evening time is "the light shall <u>not be</u> **clear." "Clear"** is defined in the Hebrew as **"valuable."** Thus, an indication that we are in the evening of this age is **"the Light [Jesus] will not be valuable."** You

11

may say that this has been happening for centuries. The answer is yes! However, there will be an increase of **"hate"** against the Light in the evening of this age.

1 John 2:9, He that says he is in the light, and hates his brother, is in darkness even until now.

*2 Thessalonians 2:3-4, ³Let no man deceive you by any means: for that day shall not come, except there comes a falling away first, and that man of sin be revealed, the son of perdition; ⁴**Who opposes and exalts himself above all that is called God**, or that is worshipped; so that he as God sits in the temple of God, shewing himself that he is God.*

*John 3:20, For everyone that **'practices'** evil hates the light, neither comes to the light, lest his deeds should be reproved.*

As one can see, a pattern of the Light being devalued was also exemplified against Jesus. Jesus also said, "Men loved darkness rather than light" (John 3:29 w/1 John 2:8). This is translated as men will give more value to "hate" rather than valuing the "love" that Jesus demonstrated. Beastly humanity will esteem the "schemed" light of Satan as more valuable than the "true Light" — Jesus.

*John 1:9-10, ⁹That was the **true Light,** which lights every man that cometh into the world. ¹⁰He was in the world, and the world was made by him, and **the world knew him not.** ¹¹ He came unto his own, and **his own received him not.***

The nations will once again devalue Jesus and act like they do not **"know him."** Jesus — the Light — came unto His own creation and they did not receive him. They acted like He has never revealed His love to their heart (Romans 1:19). The same will be true again at the evening time. **"The world"** will not consider Jesus' Light to be valuable. They will not "receive" Him as "the true Light." More value will be placed on Satan, the beast, and his false prophet, rather than on Jesus. The beast's image and his marketing practices will appear to be more valuable than the "brightness" of Jesus' "glory" (Hebrews 1:3; contrast Revelation 13).

The god of this age will also blind the nations so that they "devalue" "the light of the glorious gospel of Christ" (2 Corinthians 4:3-6). Men will choose the transformed gospel of Satan as a light <u>in lieu</u> of the Light of Jesus' gospel. Men will have the darkness of hate rather than the Light of love (John 3:19; 1 John 2:11; John 12:35). That is, mankind will choose to hate, rather than choose to love. The true Light is also a symbol of Jesus' righteousness.

With respect to the false teachers in the Church, they will teach righteousness (light) comes by paying money; and that having money is a measure of godliness (1 Timothy 6:5; see 2 Corinthians 11; 2 Corinthians 12). Many will think the transformation of Satan into light (righteousness by works) is the true Light (righteousness imparted by Jesus). When Paul made this statement with respect to Satan and his ministers' pseudo light, Paul said it in the context of false apostles traveling into the Church of Corinth preaching for money.

*2 Corinthians 11:14, 14And **no marvel;** for **Satan** himself **is transformed (Gk.: metaschematizo, to change external appearance)** into an angel of light. 15Therefore it is no great thing if his ministers also be **transformed** as the ministers of **righteousness;** whose end shall be according to their works*

Do not marvel that this will happen. Satan and his ministers will "change" the "outward appearance" of themselves into light (a form of righteousness). Men will esteem Satan's pseudo light (righteousness by works) as more valuable than Jesus' righteousness, imparted by faith. The true light being devalued is also exemplified in another form. This is seen in the book of Revelation, where "the world" will "worship the dragon … and … the beast" (Revelation 13:3-4).

That is, they worship (value) the creature **"more than"** their Creator (Romans 1:25). Satan will also change the "outward appearance" of his false apostle and ministers who will then "devalue" the true Light (Jesus) by presenting another Jesus, another gospel, and another spirit (2 Corinthians 11:4; Revelation 13:11-17). This "another gospel" will center more on corruptible men/women and their earthly desires, rather than about Jesus subduing our humiliated body to be morphed like unto His glorious body (Philippians 3: 18-21).

Paul even said that it will be possible for some in the Church to be **"removed"** into this false light (Galatians 1:6; Matthew 24:24). Just as the word **"marvel"** is associated with Satan being transformed as light, so Paul indicated that there will be a **"marvel"** towards those who are **"translated"** into the gospel of Satan that "devalue" Jesus' Light (2 Cor 11;14; Gal 1:6).

The second indication of the "evening time" is "the light shall not be ... **dark."** "Dark" is defined as **"shrink"** (see Strong's Lexicon). It is translated as **settled,** congealed, curdle, and **dark** in the King James Version. Thus, when Zechariah indicated that "the light shall **not** be ... **dark,"** this portion of the verse also states that "the light shall **not shrink."** This is powerful.

Even though some of humanity will not value **the Light (Jesus)** at the evening of this age, the Light (Jesus) will **not shrink back.** There will be a powerful manifestation of Jesus' bowls of wrath upon the authority of the dark ones (Luke 22:53; Revelation 13:2; Revelation 16:10, Revelation 16:17, Ephesians 2:2, and so on). How do the "bowls" of judgments of the last plagues relate to Jesus not shrinking back? Because "all things that are **reproved** are made manifest by the **light: for whatsoever doth make manifest is light"** (Eph. 5:13). Jesus will not shrink back; and the Saints of the Living Jesus will not shrink back. They will reprove the darkness by the Light!

*Hebrews 10:37-39, ³⁷For yet a little while, and **he that shall come will come,** and will not tarry. ³⁸Now the just shall live by faith: but if any man draws back, my soul shall have no pleasure in him. ³⁹But **we are not of them** who draw back (**lit., shrink**) unto perdition; but of them that believe to the saving of the soul.*

Jesus has no pleasure in them that **shrink** from Him, even in the time of the evening. If He has no pleasure in them that shrink back, then Jesus will not shrink back either. "The light [Jesus] shall not **shrink."**

14

There are some that believe that the Lord has "shrunk back." In the words of Peter, they "ignorantly" believe all things will continue as they were from the beginning of the creation.

The prophet, Ezekiel stated that some even falsely believe that God has loosened Himself from the earth. Thus, they falsely believe that anything goes. In the words of Jeremiah, some will falsely believe they "are delivered to do ...abominations." They do not believe that there is a real day of reckoning. They believe that Jesus will do neither good nor evil. They believe that Jesus will not "punish" (lit., visit) man's blasphemy against Him upon the earth.

Zephaniah 1:12, And it shall come to pass at that time, that I will search Jerusalem with candles, and **punish** the men that are **settled (lit., shrunk, dark)** on their lees: that say in their heart, **The LORD will not do good, neither will he do evil.**

In the evening time some will believe that the light is dark. That is, they believe that the light will shrink. They believe that "The Lord will not do good; neither will he do evil." However, Zechariah stated differently in the evening time the light will not shrink. The Lord will not be **"settled"** as Zephaniah defined "dark" or "shrink." He will **"visit the men that 'shrunk.'"**

The Lord will surely come; He will not shrink back. Jesus will "do well;" and He will also "do evil!" (Isaiah 45:7; Psalms 90:15). Neither **Jesus** nor His **"equal tribe"** will shrink back from doing the works of God because of the blasphemy of the beast (Dan. 7:11; Revelation 13:6). Jesus will not shrink back from the beast that challenges Him to war! The Lamb has subdued all, and He and His lambkin will overcome all (Revelation 17:14; 1 Peter 3:22; Revelation 19:17-21)! Jesus was born King; He is King. In fact, Jesus is the **"only** Potentate" who remains. He **is** "King of kings" (Revelation 19:16).

The third indication of the evening time is: "It shall be **one day ... not day, nor night ...** "at evening time it shall be **light."** This Scripture above is an interesting statement. I do believe that whenever the Lord Jesus comes with all His Saints in this evening time, it will not be "day, nor night" as we know it. There will be **literal "light"** at the evening time. Complimenting this truth is the fact that the word **"light"** also means **"fire"** and is translated as **"fire"** in the Scriptures.

*Malachi 1:10, Who is there even among you that would shut the doors for nothing? neither **do you kindle fire** on mine altar for nothing ….*

One of the simplest ways to understand the Scripture is to read what it says. Sometimes this means looking at a word's various meanings in the Hebrew language. As indicated above, "light" is the same Hebrew word for "fire in Malachi 1:10, cited above." Thus, "at the evening time it shall be **fire.**"

*Matthew 16:1-2, ¹The Pharisees also with the Sadducees came, and tempting desired him that he would shew them a sign from heaven. ²He answered and said unto them, when it is **evening,** ye say, it will be **fair weather:** for the sky (lit., heaven) is **red (or fiery red).***

*2 Thessalonians 1:7: And to you who are troubled rest with us, when **the Lord Jesus shall be revealed** from heaven with his mighty angels.*

*2 Thessalonians 1:8: **In flaming fire** taking vengeance on them that know not God, and that obey not the gospel of our Lord Jesus Christ:*

*2 Peter 3:4-8, ⁴And saying, **where is the promise of his coming?** for since the fathers fell asleep, all things continue as they were from the beginning of the creation. ⁵For this they willingly are ignorant of, that by the word of God the heavens were of old, and the earth standing out of the water and in the water: ⁶Whereby the world that then was, being overflowed with water, perished: ⁷But the heavens and the earth, which are now, by the same word are kept in store, reserved unto **fire** against the **day of judgment** and perdition of ungodly men. ⁸But, beloved, be not ignorant of this one thing, that **one day is with the Lord as a thousand years,** and a thousand years as one day.*

*Isaiah 66:15-16, ¹⁵For, behold, **the LORD will come with fire,** and with his chariots like a whirlwind, to render his anger with fury, and his rebuke with flames of fire. ¹⁶For **by fire and by his sword** will the LORD plead with all flesh: and the slain of the LORD shall be many.*

According to Jesus, some will be overtaken as a thief. They will misread the heavens. They will think the "fire" in "the evening time" is indicating "fair weather" for them (see Matthew16:1-2 above w/1 Thessalonians5:1-3). However, they will be overtaken by that same fire. When the promise of Jesus' coming is fulfilled, it will be a day of fire (Matthew 3:11; 1 Corinthians 3:13-15; Revelation 1:15 w/Isaiah 4:4). He will surely come with all His Saints in the flaming fire!

The fire will burn so bright that "at evening time it shall be light." The night will not be dark, and the day light will be swallowed by the fabulous light of the flaming fire of Jesus. **"For our God is a consuming fire" (Hebrews 12:29).** I believe when this sign appears, it will be too late for the unbelievers. Why?

This sign happens in one day that is only known to the Lord. Again, they will think the fiery sky means good weather on their behalf. However, they will be surprised by the reality of that fire. The Lord's Day comes an hour in which the spiritual sleepers <u>do not</u> "think" He will come. They are thinking **"fair weather;" or as the Greek word literally means, they will be thinking its good sign from (Zeus) the pseudo ruler of the air or sky** (see Thayer). However, **the mind of the coming King** is thinking "they shall not escape."

*Matthew 16:2, He answered and said unto them, when it is **evening,** ye say, it will be **fair weather:** for the sky lit., (heaven) is **red (or fiery red).***

*Zechariah 14:7, But **it shall be one day which shall be known to the LORD**, not day, nor night: but it shall come to pass, that at **evening time** it shall be light.*

*Luke 12:40, Be you therefore ready also: for the Son of man **cometh at an hour when ye think not***

*1 Thessalonians5:3, **For when they shall say, Peace and safety;** then sudden destruction cometh upon them, as travail upon a woman with child; and **they shall not escape.***

The Scriptures above are truth with qualification (compounding spiritual things with spiritual things). If one really studies the

Scriptures, one will discover that the Son of man will only come as a thief or in **"an hour when we think not"** to those who are drunkards, to those who feast excessively, to those who abuse His people, to those who are sleeping, to those who believe they can make war with Jesus and not fail, and so on. He will only come as a thief to those who cannot discern the signs of Jesus' visitations; because they refuse to believe that Jesus is the Messiah.

However, those (His brethren) who are "of the same womb" of Jesus will not be overtaken by that day as a thief! The true Church is exempt from being surprised. Jesus' command to us (the brothers/sisters of the same womb) is to: watch, guard (our) garments, and do not become shamefully naked through same-sex activity (This command is in your Bible); —the dragon, the beast, and the false prophet will recruit those "naked ones" to fight against Jesus. If we do as our King Jesus commands, we will not be recruited by false signs and we will not be surprised by Jesus when He comes as a thief in the night. Here is proof:

1 Thessalonians 5:4, But you, **brethren,** *are* **not** *in darkness, that* **that day** *should overtake you as a thief*

Paul made the statement above, not me! I am so glad that he made the statement and not me. Listen: "Brothers" literally means brothers of the same womb. So, if you came out of the **"same womb"** that Jesus, Paul, Peter, James, John, Moses, Timothy and so on came out of, He will **not** come as a thief to you. This "womb" is the womb of Jerusalem above, the mother of us all (Galatians 4:26); and the same city that mothered Moses (Hebrews 11:23; Acts 7:20). He will not come to the Saints as a thief. Why? **"You ... are not in darkness."** So, for those who say that Jesus is coming "any minute," they are essentially attempting to predict His coming as a thief to the Saints. Paul taught contrary.

Jesus will indeed come as a thief in the night to those "servants" who are sleeping (spiritually) (Luke 12:37-39; Romans 13:11 w/Romans 13:13; 1 Thessalonians 5:4, 6, 8). He will indeed come as a thief to them who trust in their own **"peace and safety"** (1 Thessalonians 5:3). He will come as a thief to those who walk in the shame of same sexuality (Revelation 16:15 w/Romans 1:27).

He will indeed come as a thief to those who have no hope in Jesus (1 Thessalonians 4:13 w/1Thessalonians 5:3). Yet, Paul stated that of the **"time and seasons"** of Jesus' coming, the Saints **"know perfectly (lit., exactly)** that the day of the Lord comes as a thief in the night" only to those who are "in darkness" (1Thessalonians 4:15-18 w/I Thessalonians 5:1-4).

It is indeed a day that is "known to **the Lord;"** and we who are **"joined to the Lord"** are also **"one spirit"** with Him (1 Corinthians 6:17). Thus, He **has** told us in His Word through **oneness** with His Holy Spirit the indications of the "exact" "times (plural)" and "seasons (plural)" of His promised coming. Notice, I did not say we will know the exact day, month, year, hour, minute, and second. That would be absurd! Yet, as we learned in the "Introduction" of this book, the Holy Spirit told Simeon that he would see the Lord's Christ before he died.

In other words, do not say He is coming in any minute **and** do not say that the Saints of the living God cannot understand by the Scriptures the times and the seasons of His coming. Jesus came the first time in the **"sunset"** of that age (Isaiah 8:22-9:2 w/Matthew 4:13-17). Yet, God made known the season of His coming in the flesh to Mary, Joseph, Zacharias, Elizabeth, Simeon, the wise men and even Herod. He also made the times and seasons of His coming known to Paul, Peter, John, and so on (2 Thessalonians2:1-3, 1 John 2; the book of Revelation). **"The LORD my God shall come, and all the saints with you ...** at **evening time**.... (Zechariah 14:5-7).

THE TABERNACLE OF TIME

*Exodus 33:7: And Moses took the tabernacle, and pitched it without the camp, afar off from the camp, and called it the **Tabernacle of the congregation. And** it came to pass, that everyone which sought the LORD went out unto the tabernacle of the congregation, which was without the camp.*

*Genesis 21:2: For Sarah conceived, and bare Abraham a son in his old age, **at the set time** of which God had spoken to him.*

Jesus in His infinite wisdom has not left His people without a way to tell time. He created time. Paul indicated that "of the times and seasons (set times)," the saints can **"know perfectly (lit., exactly)** that the day of the Lord so comes …" (2 Thessalonians 5:1-2). Thus, chronological times and set times can be ascertained through the Spirit of Jesus and the Word of God. The Word of God in Daniel 7:22 stated that **"the time came that** the saints possessed the kingdom."

Thus, just as "the time came" for Jesus to be born King; and His birth is an historical fact; so "the time came' for the saints to possess the kingdom. It will happen! Jesus will come again and give the kingdom of this world to His saints. The "times-pattern" is already established. These times can be seen in the tabernacle built by Moses.

In the verses above we see that the tent that Moses built can actually be called **"the tabernacle of the set time."** The word **"congregation"** cited in Exodus 33:7 and the phrase **"the set time"** in Genesis 21:2 are translated from the same Hebrew word "mowed" (pronounced as mo-ade); "mowed" also means "set time" or "set season." Thus, "set times" are also wrapped up "in" His Church—the "congregation" of God.

*1 Corinthians 10:11: Now all these things happened unto them for ensamples: and they are written for our admonition, **upon (Greek: "eis," into) whom the ends of the world (lit., ages) are come.***

The "ends of the ages" is a change that happens **"into"** the Church of the living God. I Corinthians 10:11 which refers to Jesus' Church actually reads "'into' whom the ends of the ages are come (the Church)." Thus, the Greek definition in 1 Corinthians 10:11c tells the story a little better. The ends of the ages have come "into" the saints. In other words, the saints have a direct impact on when and how the ages end. Again, this is also seen in the definition for the "Tabernacle of the Congregation"

Now, I do not want to encumber the reader with drawn out definitions; however, understanding time by the pattern of the tabernacle built by Moses is a vital principle in understanding God's set periods. With that said, the Hebrew word for **"congregation"** ("mowed") as defined by the Strong's Lexicon means "properly, an appointment, i.e., **a fixed time or season;** specifically, a festival; conventionally a year; by implication, an assembly (as convened for a definite purpose); technically the congregation; by extension, the place of meeting; also, a signal (as appointed beforehand)."

Therefore, the tabernacle of the congregation (or tabernacle of the set time) is a building that was also established by God as a "pattern" for His people to know God's "set times," as the Father chooses to reveal them. This is one of the reasons God admonished Moses to "make all things according to the pattern" shown to him on the mount. (Hebrews 8:5; Exodus 25:9). Moses had to be exact; because God had the **"fullness of times"** outlined in the tabernacle (see Ephesians 1:10).

In addition, according to Jesus, we will not be able to get the exact day nor hour when He comes. However, as Paul indicated, we can know **"exactly"** the "times" (<u>plural</u>) and the "seasons" (<u>plural</u>). With this in mind, let us look at the times of the ages as typified by the "tabernacle of the set time."

The tabernacle was divided into three areas (that is, three "set times") with each one of the three divisions of the tabernacle being "a fullness of time" (singular), and with all three areas comprising the "fullness of times" (<u>plural</u>) (Ephesians 1:10).

21

*Hebrews 9:2-9: ²For there was a tabernacle made; the first, wherein was the candlestick, and the table, and the showbread; which is called the sanctuary. ³And after the second veil, the tabernacle which is called the Holiest of all … ⁹Which was a figure **for the time then present (lit., the time, the present)** ….*

*Hebrews 9:2-9, NKJ: ²For **a tabernacle** was prepared: the first part, in which was the lampstand, the table, and the showbread, which is called the sanctuary… ⁹ **it was symbolic for the present time.** …*

The "tabernacle of the set time" was divided into three parts — the Outer Court, The Holy Place ("the first" — Hebrews 9:2), and The Holiest of Holies ("the second" — Hebrews 9:3). The Scripture then referred to "time" relative to the priestly functions in certain areas of the tabernacle. The practice of animal sacrifices was referred to as a "symbol for the present time" — the "present time" of the last days of animal sacrifices as abolished by Jesus' sacrifice and the "present time" of the beginning of the early Church.

After Jesus abolished sacrifices (Hebrews 10:9-10; Daniel 9:27), animal sacrifices continued (Acts 21:26; w/1 Corinthians 9:20) until they were stopped completely by the destruction of Jerusalem in A.D. 70; and when the natural Jews tried to implement it again, in A.D. 135, the Romans "ploughed" Jerusalem again. Note: this does not mean that this author is anti-Semitic or takes pleasure in the destruction of any Jew or a particular people. When my family came to America in 1975 from Jamaica West Indies, it was the Jews that took us in and showed kindness; and I still have Jewish friends. **Jesus** himself stated that Jerusalem would be destroyed in a violent way (Luke 19:41-44). It is an insult to the Father and Jesus to go back to animal sacrifice (Hebrews 10:29). As indicated above, the tabernacle built by Moses (the tabernacle of set time) was made of three areas: The Outer Court, the Holy Place, and the Holiest of Holies. The dimensions of the Outer Court are as follows: The Outer Court was one hundred (100) cubits long.

The width was fifty (50) cubits wide. The height was five (5) cubits high. Note: By looking at the dimensions of the tabernacle from different points of view, we can see different layers of truth. Thus, my point of view is not dogmatic.

Adding all the dimensions (perimeter) of the Outer Court (100 + 100 + 50 + 50 = 300 cubits) and multiplying the perimeter by the height of five (5) cubits (300 cubits x 5 cubits = 1,500 cubits). This total (1,500 cubits) is significant relative to "time." The 1,500 cubits are to be equated to 1,500 years. The Law of Moses, including, but not limited to animal sacrifices, lasted approximately 1,500 years[6] until Christ, Jesus; and animal sacrifices were abolished by the "one" sacrifice of Jesus Christ "forever."

Therefore, the writer of Hebrews defined the act of animal sacrifice by his counterparts (the Jews who did not believe "into" Jesus) as a symbol of the time then present. Even though Jesus' sacrifice did away with all other sacrifices, it actually took a few years in the natural realm to do away with animal sacrifice completely. There was an overlap between the sacrifice of Jesus that abolished all other sacrifices, and the continuance of animal sacrifices by the Jews for a season (Acts 21:26). In fact, according to the tabernacle, there are hidden overlaps between ages. Yet, the point still stands; the age of law was changed to the age of justification by faith through Jesus' blood.

Even though in the reference above (Acts 21:26), Paul participated in animal sacrifice to appease the Jews[7], he was fully aware that the sacrifice of Jesus had "abolished" animal sacrifice as outlined in the book of Galatians, Hebrews, and so on. In fact, 1 Corinthians 9:20 stated one of the reasons why Paul participated in things pertaining to the law.

Daniel also prophesied that Jesus would end animal sacrifices. The writer of Hebrews confirmed Daniel's statement and also demonstrated in certain terms that the first covenant with all its

---

[6] I learned these principles form Dr. Kelley Varner
[7] Paul from time to time would participate in certain practices of the law to appease the Jews (Acts 16:3; Acts 21:26).

animal sacrifices was then "obsolete" and "not the very image of the fact."

Hebrews 8:13, NKJ: In that He says, "A new covenant," **He has made the first obsolete.** *Now what is becoming obsolete and growing old is ready to vanish away.*

Hebrews 10:1-10: [1]For the law having a shadow of good things to come, and not the very image of the things, can never with those sacrifices which they offered year by year continually make the comers thereunto perfect. [2]For then would they not have ceased to be offered? Because that the worshippers once purged should have had no more conscience of sins… [5]Wherefore when He cometh into the world, He says, Sacrifice and offering you would not, but a body hast you prepared me: [6]In burnt offerings and sacrifices for sin you hast had no pleasure. [7]Then said I, Lo, I come (in the volume of the book it is written of me,) to do your will, O God. [8]Above when he said, Sacrifice and offering and burnt offerings and offering for sin you would not, neither had pleasure therein; which are offered by the law; [9]Then said He, Lo, I come to do your will, O God. **He takes away the first that He may establish the second.**[10]*By the which will we are sanctified through the offering of the body of Jesus Christ once for all.*

Daniel 9:27: And he shall **confirm the covenant** *with many for one week: and in the* **middle** *of the week,* **he shall cause the sacrifice and the oblation to cease** *….*

Daniel 9:27, NKJ: Then he [Jesus] shall **confirm (lit.; strengthen) a covenant** *with many for one week; But in the middle of the week,* **He shall bring an end to sacrifice and offering.**

Hebrews 8:6: but now hath he obtained a more excellent ministry, by how much also he is the mediator of **a better (lit., stronger)** *covenant, which was established upon better promises.*

The age of the law of animal sacrifices (~1,500 years) was ended by Jesus' sacrifice, and the age of "grace and truth" was begun through Jesus' work, His crucifixion, and His resurrection. It was Jesus who "strengthens a covenant" (the New Covenant) named by Daniel. The proof is found in Hebrews 8:6 where Jesus is "the Mediator of a better

(Gk.; stronger) covenant." The emphasis in the book of Hebrews is the word "stronger" (see Strong's Concordance NT #2909) which coincides with the phrase "to be strong" (Strong's Concordance OT # 1396) highlighted in Daniel 9:27. Jesus' sacrifice did indeed abolish animal sacrifice forever.

"He shall bring an end to sacrifice and offering..." This new period (covenant) of no more animal sacrifices for the Church and all humanity is also depicted by "the tabernacle of the set time." Inside the "Tent of Time" were two other sections that comprise the entire tabernacle, the Holy Place, and the Holiest of Holies.

The Holy Place was ten (10) cubits wide, twenty (20) cubits long, and ten (10) cubits high. Again, using simple mathematics: 20 x 10 x 10 =2,000 Cubits (2,000 years).

First, in this Holy Place there was no brazen altar (the place for sacrifice). Thus, there were no sacrifices in this part of the tabernacle. The Church nor anyone else is not supposed to perform animal sacrifice for forgiveness of sins in this age (2,000 years) nor "the age to come" (the day of the Lord). It is an outrage against Jesus to turn back to animals. Animal sacrifices cannot remove sin or the consciousness of sins (Hebrews 10:1-3).

Second, the Church has been in existence for approximately 2,000 years (2,000 cubits). The Church age, as we know it, will only last for approximately[8] 2,000 years. We are coming to the close of the second millennium from Jesus Christ's death, burial, and His powerful resurrection. The victorious Church is about to recognize the next dimension of the tabernacle called the day of the Lord (the thousand years rule).

In other words, the dimensions of the Holy Place are symbolic of the present duration of the Church age. It follows that the dimensions of the holiest of holies along with its furniture(s) provides the pattern of the millennium. To give a little more proof that the numbers

---

[8] We may add approximately thirty-three years for the lifetime of Jesus.

harmonize, the Holiest of Holies dimensions were 10 Cubits x 10 Cubits x 10 Cubits for a total of 1,000 Cubits. The volume of the Holiest of Holies is the same "time" as the millennium (1,000 years) to come (Revelation 20:4-6).

This is the sum of what was said so far. The dimensions of the outer court of the tabernacle built by Moses were approximately the same time that the age of the law lasted, as taught by Dr Kelley Varner. This was depicted by summing the outer perimeter of the tabernacle and multiplying the sum of the perimeter by the height of the outer court [(100+100+50+50) x 5=1,500 cubits (years)].

Note: The author realizes that the method used for finding this measurement for the Outer Court differs from the method used of the Holy Place and Most Holy Place where he uses the volume to arrive at 2,000 and 1,000 cubits/years, respectively. However, the reader must consider that the outer court is uncovered, so volume may not be the most appropriate measurement, and that the age of the law is inherently different from the age of grace, which may also account for why the calculation is handled differently.

The dimensions of the Holy Place speak to the current age of the Church which we are presently experiencing, as taught by Dr Kelley Varner. We are currently ~2,000 years from Christ's death, burial, and His powerful resurrection. Again, looking at the dimensions of the Holy Place we see that the "volume" of that area is 2,000 cubits (20 cubits long x 10 cubits high x 10 cubits wide=2,000 cubits (years). The numbers harmonize with the present duration of the Church. The end of the age is closer than we realize.

Daniel indicated in Daniel 7:22 that **"the time came** for the saints to possess the kingdom." "The time came" for Jesus to come in the flesh approximately 2,000 years ago to end the age of atonement by animal sacrifice. That is "the time came" for the Church age to commence with redemption being realized by Jesus' "stronger blood." It follows that according to Daniel 7:22, "the time came" for the saints to possess the kingdom, which appears to be the 1,000 years millennium rule.

The Church will "possess the kingdom" of the world (Revelation 11:15). This will happen during the next phase of the times and seasons the Father has put in His own power. It will be the time of the millennium with the understanding that there will be an overlap of the ages before the millennium rule is realized. The Holy of Holies was dimensioned as 10 cubits x 10 cubits x 10 cubits, which equals 1,000 cubits (years). The volume of the Holiest place in the Tent of Time gives a pattern of the millennium—1,000 years (see Revelation 20:4-5). These one thousand years is the day of the Lord. It is also known as the "age to come."

A DAY, AN AGE

*2 Peter 3:18: But grow in grace, and in the knowledge of our Lord and Savior Jesus Christ. To him be glory both now **and forever.** Amen.*

Jesus' grace and knowledge is the environment in which we "grow." This growth is realized as we recognize His saving Lordship and His salvaging of our spirit, soul, and bodies. Peter stated this encouragement directly after discussing the coming of Jesus, or the coming of the day of the Lord (2 Peter 3:3-4; 8-10).

Peter then concludes his encouragement to the saints to grow by saying that the "glory" of this growth is **"to [Jesus] forever."** The word **"forever"** reads in the Greek texts as **"into a day, an age."** It appears that from this statement, in context of the entire Chapter of 2 Peter 3, the **thousand years** "day of the Lord," or **"a day"** is defined as **"an age."**

This ("age"), I believe, is what the Bible calls the **"age to come"** (Hebrews 6:5) or what our Lord Himself calls **"that age"** (Luke 20:34). The length of this "day" from God's perspective is the key to seeing this "day of the Lord," as "an **age"**

That is, what is the duration of God's day? How long is an age? As indicated a previous chapter, Peter gave the answer. The day of the Lord is not just one of "man's days," as we know it. One of the Lord's Days is one thousand years for us.

 In 2 Peter 3, Peter's subject was "the promise of his coming." (2 Peter 3:3-4). Peter then referred to some past events which confirmed that Jesus will indeed come again to judge the heavens and the earth. Just as the "time came" for the **first world;** the "time came" for this present **second world.** He cited a cataclysm of the heavens and earth by water, a cataclysm which the "scoffers" willingly forgot (2 Peter 3:3; 6).

He then said that "the heavens and the earth, which are now," would also face another cataclysm of fire through Jesus' coming (2 Peter 3:7-

13, 2 Thessalonians 1:7-10). In addition, with respect to the promise of Jesus' coming, Peter called it the "day of the Lord" and the "day of judgment (lit., crisis)."

*2 Peter 3:7-8: ⁷But the heavens and the earth, which are now, by the same word are kept in store, reserved unto fire against the day of judgment and perdition of ungodly men. ⁸But, beloved, be not ignorant of this one thing, that **one day** is with the Lord as **a thousand years, and a thousand years as one day.***

*2 Peter 3:10: But the **day of the Lord** will come as a thief in the night....*

This **"day** of Judgment" or **"day** of the Lord" makes for an interesting study. This "day," as it turns out, is really **1,000 years.** This is the one thousand (1, 000) years period that is also called the "age to come," or "that age." Proof! In the next verse, 2 Peter 3:8, Peter clarified the **"day** of judgment" <u>as</u> 1,000 years. Thus, one can understand Peter's phrase "a day, an age" at the end of the same chapter in which he defined the length of God's day. God's "day" (1,000 years) is also an "age".

Our day consists of twenty-four (24) hours; however, God's day consists of one thousand (1,000) years). In other words, "one hour" in God's day is approximately forty-two years (42 years) in man's timetable. God's hour hand on His clock may not change to the next hour until after forty-two years. Again, for emphasis, this "age" of 1, 000 years is also called "a day." Listen to the learned apostle of the Lamb.

2 Peter 3:7-8: ⁷But the heavens and the earth, which are now, by the same word are kept in store, reserved unto fire against the day of judgment and perdition of ungodly men. ⁸But, beloved, be not ignorant of this one thing, that one day is with the Lord as a thousand years, and a thousand years as one day.

Peter said "do not be ignorant" about how long this "day of Judgment" really is! According to Peter, this "day" is 1,000 years. Saying it another way, the promise of His coming is the event that will implement His millennium rule of one day showing that Jesus is indeed the only dynasty. This makes His "day" or "coming" a little different from previously thought. The "day of Judgment" is the "age" of the millennium.

This "day" (1,000 years) begins after the resurrection of the "first-fruit Christ," which is a course of "the first resurrection," and concludes "when He shall have delivered up the kingdom to God, even the Father … that God may be all in all" (see 1 Corinthians 15:24-28, Revelation 20:4-6). Again, this is what Peter also called "a day, an age." And according to Peter, it is an era **"into"** which Jesus Christ receives "glory." "To him **be glory** both now and **'into a day an age.'** Amen" (2 Peter 3:18).

Paul said we are changed "out of" one dimension of glory "into" glory (The Holy Spirit, Jesus' life, Jesus' righteousness, etc.). We have the glory of Jesus "now;" and Jesus will extend that "glory…into a day an age." That is, we glorify Jesus "now," as Peter said; and by pressing "into the age" of the Holy of Holies where our forerunner Jesus sits, we will also show off Jesus' glory in that age.

With that said, we now know that the coming millennium is also called the "day of the Lord." If the coming millennium is called the "day of the Lord," what were the other "days" (millennia) called? The Holy Writ distinguished between the "day of the Lord" and the "day of man." However, the Lord will do more in His day than mankind has done in all their "days" (6,000 years).

2 Peter 3:10: But the day of the Lord will come as a thief in the night; in the which the heavens shall pass away with a great noise, and the elements shall melt with fervent heat, the earth also and the works that are therein shall be burned up.

*1 Corinthians 4:3-5: ³But with me it is a very small thing that I should be judged of you, or of **man's judgment (lit., man's day):** yea, I judge not mine own self… ⁵Therefore judge nothing before the time, until the Lord come, who both will bring to light the hidden things of darkness, and will make manifest the counsels of the hearts: and then shall every man have praise of God.*

The words **"man's judgment"** is literally translated from the Greek as **"man's day."** Paul distinguishes between being judged by "man's day" and being judged in the Lord's Day when Jesus "comes." According to Peter, Jesus' "coming" is called the "day of the Lord." Thus, Paul distinguished between "man's day" and "the Lord's day."

Man's day is typified by mankind who likes to "judge" things **"before the time." This** can be characterized by prejudices (prejudgments) that have arisen in all races. This can be typified judgment upon a person without due process. "Man's day" did this to Jesus. They sentenced Him to death even before they heard His defense (John 7:51).

In addition, "man's day" refers to the **6,000 years** of man's **"untimely"** criterion of "judging ... before time" in the earth. Adam made a judgment (decision) without consulting the Lord in the **"spirit of the [Lord's] day."** That is, he decided to eat from the wrong tree, before the Lord came and walked with him in "the spirit of the [Sabbath] day." For those who do not know this, Adam was created on the "sixth day." However, Adam sinned on the Sabbath day.

Thus, the number for man is **six (6).** We are six thousand years **(6,000 years)** or six days from the first Adam. These "six days" are the days that unregenerate man has been judging in the earth outside the "spirit of the Lord's day." This untimely judgment has been going on for six (6) days, or six thousand years.

This is a true statement; because Peter says that one day equals one thousand years. Six (6) is also seen in the number of the beast, the number of the beast's name is 666 (man's complete blasphemy against God) (Revelation 13:1-17). Man's day is the age (6,000 years) when the number of the beast is also the criterion for those who sit to misjudge. It is a day in which man's judgment has excluded God from the judicial systems. "Because of man," the number of the beast became the criterion for doing business in the unjust market systems of the world (Revelation 13:16-18).

31

The beast' **criterion** for buying and selling is a person must participate in beast worship; a person must mark himself/herself with the character of the beast, the name of the beast or the number of the beast. Breach of the beast's marketing criterion is death.

The day of the Lord, in contrast to man's criteria, is a day, or an age of His righteous criteria. As we have lived in man's day, some shall also live in **God's day**, "the age to come." It will be an age in which "righteousness" will dwell in the heavens and in the earth. And, for those who can receive it, we can live in that age, now.

We live in the heavenly places, now (Ephesians 2:6; Philippians 3:20; 2 Peter 3:13). Inheriting God's incorruptible kingdom is future, yet the kingdom of God is a very present reality as defined by Jesus (Matthew 12:28, Luke 10:9, Luke 11:20). The kingdom of God "squeezes" us like a "throttle," now. Yes, we can also taste the same age Jesus is currently living in!

*Hebrews 6:5: and have **tasted** the good word of God, <u>and</u> the **powers of the world** to come.*

*Hebrews 6:5, NKJ: And have **tasted** the good word of God <u>and</u> the **powers of the age** to come.*

We can see from the verses above that we can **"taste** … the powers of the age to come." In other words, whenever that age is, we can live there now! The "age to come" is the "Today" in Christ (see Hebrews 4). It is a place (Holy of Holies) called "forever." It is "the age" we must be carried "into." Saying it yet another way, we can live in the power of the millennial age, now!

"That age" is the place where Jesus is, now. We can live "into the age," now! We can live "in the Spirit of the Lord's day (age)," now! Our forerunner is seated there and waiting for some to enter in. This age is the "Today" of "Sabbatism" (Hebrews 4:6-7; 4:9; 6:19-20 [see Greek definitions]).

This Sabbatism is a person—Jesus; and the Sabbatism will also be a literal day—the millennial rule with the Christ. It is a day; an age, when mankind is to cease from man's works of 666 and enter into Jesus' **rest, "the Sabbatism"** (Hebrews 4:10; Revelation 20). It is a day, an age when it is lawful to do good and unlawful to do evil (Mark 3:4). And according to the Holy Bible, we can experience that age now.

With that said, as surely as Jesus came the first time, He shall come again in His saints and with all the saints. It is a historical truth that Jesus came the first time; and it is a powerful truth that He will yet come again, physically. As surely as man's day exists, the "day of the Lord" is dawning on mankind.

Jesus, who "made the ages," came two thousand years ago and "framed (lit., mended, repaired) the ages" that were damaged by man's day. (Hebrews 1:2 with Hebrews 11:3). He will yet come again to be glorified in His saints by resurrecting those who are counted worthy to obtain that age of Sabbath (the rest of the Lord's Day).

Hosea 6:2: After (lit., from) two days will he revive us: in the third day He will raise us up, and we shall live in his sight.

First, we are "two days" from Jesus' death, burial, resurrection, and ascent. That is, as Peter imparted to us his understanding of God's time, we are two thousand years from Jesus' death, burial, resurrection, and ascent. Saying it another way, according to Peter's reckoning of time, we are two ages from Jesus' death, burial, resurrection, and ascent.

It is "in" these past two days (or two thousand years) that Jesus is "reviving" us (His Church). He has/is "mending" the ages. In addition, **"in the day, the third"** (**the third one thousand years from Jesus'** death, burial, resurrection, and ascent) He "will raise us up, and we shall live in His sight." This "third day" is the thousand years mentioned by Peter and John, the beloved. It is the day of His rest in His resurrection life.

In other words, the Day of the Lord is an age of resurrection (Luke 20:35). This day is three days from Jesus (the last Adam), or seven days from the first Adam. This third day is **"the age about to be."** It is "the age" of His "day" of rest. Thus, in light of Peter's impartation to us that God's day is one thousand years, the verse above could read like this:

"After two [thousand years] He will make us live; in the third [one thousand years], He will raise us up, and we shall live in His sight." Does this sound like Revelation 20:4? Does this look like the Holy Place (2,000 cubits (years)) and the Holy of Holies (1,000 cubits (years)) in the Tent of Time, as patterned by Moses.

*Revelation 20:4-6: ⁴And I saw thrones, and they sat upon them, and judgment was given unto them: and I saw the souls of them that were beheaded for the witness of Jesus, and for the word of God, and which had not worshipped the beast, neither his image, neither had received his mark upon their foreheads, or in their hands; and they lived and reigned with Christ **a thousand years.** ⁵But the rest of the dead lived not again until the thousand years were finished. This is the first resurrection.⁶Blessed and holy is he that hath part in the first resurrection: on such the second death hath no power, but they shall be priests of God and of Christ and shall reign with him **a thousand years.***

The millennium is "a day, an age." It is the day of the Lord. It is defined as the age of the first resurrection of the "blessed and holy." It is defined as the "day" when the resurrected "rule <u>with</u> Christ a thousand years," or "one day" according to Peter.

It is defined as the rule of Melchizedek (Jesus) and His priesthood. That is when those who have joined Jesus "into the age" will serve as priests "with" (near) Him (Hebrews 6:19-20; 2 Peter 2:9; 2 Peter 3:10; Revelation 20:4 last part w/Revelation 20:6). It is the realization of the heavenly dimensions of the Holy of Holies as defined by Moses. It is the age, the day "into" which God will be **"glorified."**

*2 Peter 3:18: But grow in grace, and in the knowledge of our Lord and Savior Jesus Christ. To him be **glory** both now and forever (lit., **into a day, an age**). Amen.*

THE TENTH MONTH—300 DAYS

Esther 2:16-17: So, Esther was taken unto king Ahasuerus into his house royal in the **tenth month,** *which is the month* **Tebeth,** *in the seventh year of his reign.*

Exodus 36:8-9: [8]*And every wise hearted man among them that wrought the work of the tabernacle made ten curtains of fine twined linen, and blue, and purple, and scarlet: with cherubim of cunning work made he them.*[9]*The length of one curtain was* **twenty and eight cubits,** *and the breadth of one curtain four cubits: the curtains were all of one size.*

Exodus 36:14-15: [14]*And he made curtains of goats' hair for the tent over the tabernacle: eleven curtains he made them.* [15]*The length of one curtain was* **thirty cubits,** *and four cubits was the breadth of one curtain: the eleven curtains were of one size.*

Jesus is King, now! In the book of Esther, King Ahasuerus typifies Jesus, especially with respect to Jesus' sovereignty. Esther was chosen instead of Vashti, as the Church (the Israel of God made up of Jews and Gentiles) is chosen instead of natural Israel. King Ahasuerus had divorced Vashti, even though it was against Persian customs of that day to call the queen for display before drunken men.

Another queen had to be chosen. Thus, many virgins were prepared to go unto the king **"in the evening"** to be chosen by name (Esther 2:14). "The time came" for each to go to the king after twelve months of "purifications."

The time came in evening of "the tenth month" for Esther to be "taken" to the king. "The tenth month" is significant relative to the "translation" of some from this age (man's day) "into the age." This will be developed relative to the linen[9] curtains that were underneath

---

[9] Linen is symbolic of Jesus' righteous acts imparted to His saints; and also, the fulfillment of Jesus' righteous acts through the saints (Rev 19:8; Rom 8:4; w/Phil 3:9).

the outer cover of the Tabernacle of the Congregation or the Tabernacle of the Set Time.

We will look at the curtains of the Tabernacle of Time relative to the "tenth month" as outlined in the book of Esther. This "tenth month" occurred "in the seventh year" of King Ahasuerus' reign, this may prophetically point to a 300-year period relative to the seventh one thousand years from the first Adam.

With that said, the curtains in the Tabernacle of Set Time also reveal events in God's time as does the Tabernacle as whole. This book has already discussed the dimensions of the tabernacle that Moses built for the Lord. We saw how the Holy Place (Church Age) was admeasured to be approximately 2,000 cubits (years). The Most Holy (the millennium) was calculated to be approximately 1,000 cubits (years).

In like manner, the curtains of the tabernacle cited at the beginning of this chapter, will be used to show that there is a transition between the two ages — the existing Church age and the "day of the Lord" to come, also called by some, the millennial rule with Christ. I call this transition the overlap.[10] Sometime during this transition there will be a **translation** of some "into the age" where Jesus now sits.

Note: I do not claim to know the exact date when this overlap started; nor when it will end. Neither do I claim to know the exact beginning "in the tenth month in the seventh year" when the Church of the firstborn is to be "taken" into the age to come and "the greatness of the kingdom under the whole heaven, shall be given to the people of the saints of the Most High." Remember how God told Abraham that his seed would remain in Egypt 400 years? Yet, it was actually 430 years.

---

[10] Please refer to one of my books titled, *The Last Hour, The First Hour, The 42nd Generation* for additional details.

Remember, Jeremiah's vision of 70 years captivity was expanded to be 490 years in Daniel 9. God is sovereign. His sovereignty over time also extends into our age and the age to come. When we look at the Tabernacle of Time, there is always more than meets "our time."

Yet Jesus is so wonderful that He gives His holy apostles and prophets a glimpse into His mysteries for the ages to be imparted to His saints (Revelation 1:1). In one of the Scriptures cited at the beginning of this chapter (Exodus 36:9), there were **ten curtains, four cubits wide**, which covered the tabernacle.

*Exodus 36:8-9: [8]And every wise hearted man among them that wrought the work of the tabernacle made **ten curtains** of fine twined linen, and blue, and purple, and scarlet: with cherubim of cunning work made he them.[9]The length of one curtain was **twenty and eight cubits**, and the breadth of **one curtain four cubits**: the curtains were all of one size.*

*Exodus 36:14-15: [14]And he made curtains of goats' hair for the tent over the tabernacle: eleven curtains he made them. [15]The length of one curtain was **thirty cubits**, and four cubits was the breadth of one curtain: **the eleven curtains** were of one size.*

When they are coupled together, they total forty (40) cubits. This applies to the length of the tabernacle. However, these particular linen curtains were only 28 cubits long compared to the 30 cubits needed to cover the entire walls of the Tabernacle as the outer covering did. This (28 cubits) is significant.

Looking at the front of the tabernacle, the width of the Tabernacle, coupled with the height of both sides of the tabernacle were 30 cubits long (10+10+10=30). Thus, the measurement of 28 cubits (9+10+9=28) indicates that this linen curtain rests approximately one (1) cubit from the bottom of the tabernacle.

Let us look at some simple math: (30-28=2), then divide the two (2) cubits into equal parts for both sides). The two (2) equal parts are one (1) cubit each.

The same is true of the entire tabernacle (the Holy Place and the Most Holy). The entire length, plus the covering for the height of the back of the tabernacle, equals forty cubits (30 +10=40). However, because this particular curtain is held one cubit off the floor at the sides, to keep the curtain uniform, the back also will be held above the ground by one (1) cubit which means that the front had an overhang of one (1) cubit.

This overhang of one (1) cubit can speak to the overlap of Jesus' age (time on earth) that must be considered when considering the additional forty years that accrued before animal sacrifices were completely stopped.

With the above statements in mind, let us give the significance of the 40 x 28 in relation to **"the tenth month" of Esther's experience.** In a previous chapter, we learned that the ages of God relative to His people are "patterned" by the tabernacle. The past two thousand years (the current Church ages) are reckoned by 10 x 10 x 20=2,000 cubits (years). Thus, the measurements of all the curtains also relate to "time" pertaining to the Church. With respect to the linen curtain, three hundred cubits (300 cubits/years) becomes significant.

Now with the width of the curtain being 28 cubits, the dimensions ("durations") is now calculated to be **10 cubits wide x 9 cubits high x 20 cubits long=1800[11] cubits (years).** This points to a 200 years difference (overlap) between the "ends" of the two curtains (the linen curtain and the goats' hair covering). The other curtain of "goat's hair," being 44 cubits long, could have an overlap of 4 cubits at the front of the tabernacle (Exodus 36:14-15). Thus, the 40 cubits left over from the 44 cubits (44-4=40 cubits)[12] would fit over the length of the assembled tabernacle perfectly.

The millennium is demonstrated by 10 x 10 x 10=1,000 cubits (years). However, with this curtain being shorter, the dimensions now calculate to be 9 x 10 x 10=900 cubits (years). This shows a difference

---

[11] A study of the 1800s will yield significant historical events relative to the Church.
[12] This can be developed further in reference to Jesus' lifetime on earth.

of 100 years from the 1,000 years. Either one hundred years before the new millennium starts, or the first one hundred years in the new millennium, there will be a transition between the kingdom of men and the kingdom of God.

In the words of Daniel "the time came" for the saints to possess the kingdom. The 200 years of the last part of the two thousand years from Jesus, plus the 100 years of the first part of the millennium years total 300 years. These 300 years relate to "the tenth month in the seventh year" in the book of Esther. These 300 years are patterned as follows: The "tenth month" means that ten (10) months have passed in that year, 10 months of 30 days per month of a 360 days-year; thus, $10 \times 30 = 300$ days (years).

The overlap of the ages may be marked by 300 years! Enoch was translated not to see death after he walked with God for 300 years. He did this **around the end of the first millennium.** So likewise, at the end of the sixth (6th) millennium, overlapping the start of the seventh (7th) millennium, I believe there will be a transfiguring, a transition and translation being realized similarly to the manner in which Jesus, Paul and John experienced it.

Some will have the ability to migrate between heaven and the natural realm by transfiguration. Jesus did this! Some who are counted worthy will also be "carried through" into the age to come. Some may say this is impossible. However, remember that all things are possible with God (Mark 14:36).

*Matthews 17:1-2: ¹And **after six days** Jesus takes Peter, James, and John his brother, and brings them up into a high mountain apart, ²And was **transfigured** before them: and his face did shine as the sun, and his raiment was white as the light.*

*2 Corinthians 12:2: I knew a man in Christ above fourteen years ago, **(whether in the body, I cannot tell; or whether out of the body, I cannot tell:** God knows) such a one caught up to the third heaven.*

Revelation 22:8-9: ⁸And I John saw these things and heard them. And when I had heard and seen, I fell down to worship before the feet of the angel which *showed me these things. ⁹Then says he unto me, see you do it not: for **I am your fellow servant, and of your brethren the prophets,** and of them which keep the sayings of this book: worship God.*

As, the Scriptures above indicate, men have and will be able to migrate between two realms.[13] That is, Jesus was able to change His body into a glorified body (heavenly), and then change back to His original state. Jesus through His birthright—the right to birth it first—was the first to transfigure **on the earth,** "after six days." If you can receive it, **"after six days"** is symbolic of a period "after" six thousand years in which there will be other transfigurations and translations.

Jesus was not physically removed from the earth like Enoch and Elijah when he was "made different" in transfiguration. Jesus' change happened right here on the earth. Moses and Elijah who appeared on the mount with Jesus exemplified those who were glorified, and yet could manifest in the natural, as God willed. Paul, in like manner, did not know if he was in the body (natural realm) or out of the body (spiritual realm) when he met a man who had been "seized" to Paradise. The same happened to John in the book of Revelation; He "became" in the Spirit on the Lord's day" (not Sunday, but the Lord's day, the seventh millennium). In the Spirit he saw many angels. Yet, the angel that John spoke with in the Spirit was apparently a prophet.

Also, there will be some like Enoch. They will be completely translated as part of their birthright as part of the witness of the "resurrection" power of Jesus. I believe this may happen towards the "end" of the three hundred years overlap between this age and the next age. It may also happen again towards the "end" of the **seventh millennium,** whenever God determines that "end" to be. This is also exemplified by Esther who was "in type" translated to the "king's" royal house **in the tenth month in the seventh year** of King Ahasuerus (a type of King Jesus).

---

[13] A restoration of what was once restricted from Adam.

40

Please be reminded that the "seventh year" also prophetically points to the Sabbatism of Jesus' rest that is experienced now though faith in Jesus (Hebrews 4:3; 9-10). The tenth month points to approximately 300 days into the year; and 300 is the symbolic number for "translation" from the earthly dimension to the heavenly dimension.

*Genesis 5:24: And Enoch walked with God: and he was not; for God **took him**.*

*Hebrews 11:5: By faith Enoch was **translated** that he should not see death; and was not found, because God had translated him....*

*Genesis 2:15: And the LORD God **took ["translated"14]** the man and put him into the garden of Eden to dress it and to keep it.*

*Esther 2:16: So, Esther was **taken ["translated"]** unto king Ahasuerus into his house royal in the tenth month, which is **the month Tebeth,** in the seventh year of his reign.*

God **"took"** Enoch. This word "took" is defined as "translated" in Hebrews 11:5. Thus, Enoch was translated that he should not see death. God did the same to Adam. "God **took** the man" or in the understanding of the New Testament, "God **'translated'** the man ... into the Garden of Eden." The Garden of Eden is defined as "the third heaven" in the New Testament (2 Corinthians 12:2, 2 Corinthians 12:4, Revelation 2:7, Genesis 3:24). Thus, Adam was taken from the earth realm to the heavenly realm. Adam lived in both heaven and earth.

The same happened to Esther in the tenth month, in the seventh year. Esther was **"taken" (translated)** unto the king." As indicated earlier, the tenth month is the tenth 30 day[15] cycle in a 360-day year. Therefore, in type, Esther was "taken" (translated) on the 300th day in the seventh year. She was translated to the King in seventh year. This can represent the Church being translated into the seventh

---

[14] I can insert "translated" here because the word "took" used in Genesis 5:24 is also interpreted as "translated" in the Septuagint, the Bible that Jesus and the apostles used.
[15] Please note that the 30 days assigned to each month is an approximation.

41

millennium of God's rest or translated into the spiritual "Sabbatism" of God through faith in Jesus).

*Hebrews 4:3-10, ³For we which have **believed** do enter into rest, …. ⁹There remains therefore a **rest (lit., Sabbatism)** to the people of God. ¹⁰For he that is entered into his rest, he also hath ceased from his own works, as God did from his.*

Esther ceased from her own works by "believing" in the Eunuch's instruction as to how to prepare to meet the King. She then entered the king's rest typified by the "seventh year" of the king's rule and became queen. That is, she ruled with her King. With respect to the 300 cubits (years) overlap of the tabernacle curtains, the transition towards the seventh year (the seventh one thousand years from the first Adam, began around A.D. 1800).

Even though "outwardly" the goats' hair extended to the entirety of the ages (the Church age of 2,000 cubits (years) and the "Day of the Lord" (1,000 cubits (years)), **"from the inside"** of the tabernacle **the linen** underneath the goats' hair can **represent the beginning of 300 years transition.** This difference of 300 years could only be seen from the "inside." The linen was only fully seen from the inside by the Levites who set up the tabernacle, the high priests (Jesus in type), and the high priests' sons (Jesus' sons). Saying it another way, those who were "partakers" of the Tabernacle of the Congregation (or Tabernacle of the Set Time) saw the linen.

In New Testament language, the transition from one age to another age can be understood by those who are imparted with the fine white linen of Jesus' righteousness. The 1800s (which just happen to be approximately 300 years after Martin Luther's reformation) mark a significant rebuilding of the Church who by **"grace reign through righteousness (white linen) unto eternal life by Jesus Christ our Lord"** (Romans 5:21). Even though the 1800s were marked by the birthing of many strange doctrines, Jesus was still working a transition by His righteous acts in His people.

This season is to last approximately ten (10) months — 300th day of the year. This is typified in the tenth month that was Esther's "turn" or "order" to see the king. In addition, when Esther's "turn" (lit., "order") came, the Holy Writ stated that Esther was also "taken." In the understanding of the New Testament through Old Testament types, during Esther's "order," she was "translated" to King Jesus' house of ruling.

*Esther 2:15: Now when the **turn (lit., order, succession)** of Esther, the daughter of Abihail the uncle of Mordecai, who had taken her for his daughter, was come to go in unto the king, she required nothing but what Hegai the king's chamberlain, the keeper of the women, **appointed (lit., say)** ...*

Esther had an "order" as seen in the Hebrew definition above. It is the "order of Melchizedek." Here is proof: Melchizedek was "without father, without mother, without descent..." (Hebrews 7:3). Esther "had neither father nor mother" (Esther 2:7); and with respect to "descent," Esther was not of the "descent" of the Persians and Medes. Esther's parents were dead, and she was a Jewess. Esther is a type of the Church (a woman) who is of the "order" of Melchizedek (Jesus). Like Melchizedek and Esther, we do not belong to the lineage of the Aaron's priesthood. However, because of faith in Jesus, we are now of Jesus' royal lineage. This is true for women also. They too are in the Melchizedek order. According to the Bible, women will have an important role in this age and the age to come (Numbers 27:1-11, Psalms 68:11, Acts 2:17, Acts 18:24-26, Ruth, Galatians 3:28).

"The time came" for "the 'order' of Esther ... to go in unto the king ...." This time is[16] "in the tenth month" (a 300-year period from an unknown "beginning" in the 1800s[17] until ...). If you can receive it,

---

[16] The tenth month also has importance to a time in the Sabbath (7th) millennium. This event with Esther (a type of the Church of Jesus) happened during the tenth month in **the seventh year,** which may point to the tenth season of the seventh millennium, which may reach as far as 833 years into the 7th millennium.

[17] Note: This author **is not** referring to the beginning of the erroneous teachings of the Seventh Day Adventist, Mormonism, Jehovah's Witnesses, rapture theory and so on that began in the early 1800s.

sometime in the 1800s is the beginning of transition into the Sabbatism of Jesus' finished work of rulership with respect to the Church understanding <u>again</u> that the rule of Jesus' righteousness (linen) is unto eternal life (Romans 5:21).

*Romans 5:21: That as sin hath reigned unto death, even so **might grace reign** through righteousness unto eternal life by Jesus Christ our Lord.*

It is His righteousness (linen curtain) that works "eternal" changes in us. Through His offering for our sins (goats' hair) He works eternal changes in the "atoms" and "eye" of us. It is Jesus who will "subdue" (change) the body of this humiliation to be conformed to His glorious body. These changes in the "atoms" and "eyes" are also accomplished through the voice of the seventh or last trumpet.

In the seventh year (the seventh one thousand years from the first Adam), King Jesus (typified by king Ahasuerus[18]) will be presented with His "virgin" (Church of the firstborns) who will be "changed" and **"taken"** to Him "into the age" as Melchizedek (King of Righteousness) was "carried through" "into the age." Now note: In the tenth month she was **"taken** … into his [the king's] house royal" (Est. 2:16). The Church is called a **"royal** priesthood" (2 Peter 2:9); with the **"royal law"** (James 2:8).

This "house royal" or literally "house of kingdom," or "house of dominion" or "house of rule" points to the "rule" of our Melchizedek (Jesus) and His order "into the age" of the millennium to come. Jesus is the "High Priest" (Melchizedek); and the true Church (Esther in type) is the royal priests. Yes! He is King now. Yes! We are priests now. Yes, there will be a coming of the Lord "in" us in the evening of this age, and the kingdom of the world will also be **"translated"** into His kingdom to be shepherded by Jesus our High Priest and all His priestly saints with Him. The tenth month (complete deliverance

---

[18] The Persian meaning of Ahasuerus is mighty man or mighty eye (Bible Works BDB Hebrew Lexicon (Whittaker)).

from death) in the seventh thousand years (the year of rest) will come; "the time came."

*Daniel 7:22: … the Ancient of days came, and judgment was given to the saints of the Most High; and **the time came that the saints possessed the kingdom.***

*Revelation 20:6: Blessed and holy is he that hath part in the first resurrection: on such the second death hath no power, but they shall be **priests of God and of Christ and** shall reign with him a **thousand years.***

*1 Peter 2:9: But you are a chosen generation, a **royal priesthood,** a holy nation, a peculiar people….*

*Hebrews 6:19-20: [19]Which hope we have as an anchor of the soul … which enters into that within the veil; [20]Whither the forerunner is for us entered, even Jesus, made a **high priest forever (lit., a High Priest into the age)** after the order of **Melchizedek.***

*Esther 2:16-17: So, Esther was taken unto king Ahasuerus into his house royal in the tenth month, which is the month Tebeth, **in the seventh year of his reign.***

The verses above speak for themselves. Yet, for those who believe that a translation without death is impossible, for those who disbelieve that the Lord's kingdom is filling the earth and will rule the empire of the earth in the millennium to come, listen to the Holy Writ: "Elias was a man subject to **like passions** as we are…" (James 5:17); and "… Elijah went up by a whirlwind into heaven" (2 Kings 2:11).

Elijah was just like us. He had a nature like ours. Yet **God "took"** Elijah to the invisible dimension(2 Kings 2:5). Remember now, Elijah was intimidated by a false prophetess (Jezebel); yet he was not disqualified for translation into heaven for his fear of a witch.

The problem is that people think that they have to do the work; therefore, they disbelieve; because they feel their nature disqualifies them. Not true! We must "cease from [our own works" and "'**use speed'** to enter His rest" (Hebrews 4:10-11). Elijah has a "nature" like ours, yet the Lord took him up.

45

God is the one who initiates a translation from one dimension to another, not man. It is **Jesus** who "shall change our vile body, that it may be fashioned like unto His glorious body, according to the working whereby **He** is able even to subdue all things unto Himself" (Philippians 3:21). Adam was translated by the "Lord God." Enoch was taken by "God," Elijah was taken into heaven by the "Lord." It was Jesus who "took" the three disciples to witness Jesus' transfiguration.

Matthew 17:1-2: [1]*And after six days **Jesus takes** Peter, James, and John his brother, and brings them up into a high mountain apart,* [2]*and was transfigured before them…*

*2 Kings 2:1, NKJ: And it came to pass, when the **LORD** was about to take up Elijah into heaven by a whirlwind, that Elijah went with Elisha from Gilgal.*

*Genesis 5:24, NKJ: and Enoch walked with God; and he was not, for **God** took him.*

Do you see it? All you have to do is know that God will do the work. The Lord said, we cannot change one cubit to our height, and we cannot make one of our hairs white or black. It will be **Jesus** "Who will transform our lowly body that it may be conformed to His glorious body …" (Philippians 3:21).

 It will be Jesus who will "preserve [us] unto his heavenly kingdom" (2 Timothy 4:18). In the evening of this age, in the 300 years, and in the seventh thousand years from the first Adam, the Lord shall translate those who have discarded their "own works" for righteousness and have held on to **Jesus' righteousness (Jesus' linen)** into the age of His rest. They have experienced the **"fellowship of His suffering;"** and thus they shall reign with Him in the first resurrection of those who will be raised **"'out of' the dead."**[19] Amen! So be it!

---

[19] Philippians 3:9-11; 2 Timothy 2:12

THE TWO ENDS

Exodus 25:18-20: [18]*And you shall make two cherubim of gold of beaten work shall you make them, in* **the two ends of the mercy seat.** [19]*And make one cherub on the one end, and the other cherub on the other end: even of the mercy seat shall you make the cherubim on* **the two ends** *thereof.* [20]*And the cherubim shall stretch forth their wings on high, covering the mercy seat with their wings, and their faces shall look one to another; toward the mercy seat shall the faces of the cherubim be.*

John 20:11-12: [11]*But Mary stood without at the* **sepulcher** *weeping: and as she wept, she stooped down, and looked into the sepulcher,* [12] *and sees* **two angels in white sitting,** *the* **one at the head,** *and the* **other at the feet,** *where the body of Jesus had lain.*

Jesus is the Mercy Seat which can be seen by comparing the Scriptures above. Thus, before I develop "the two ends" fully, I want to take time to show Jesus as our living Mercy Seat with the two living cherubim. In the book of John cited above, a beautiful "living" reality shows the Mercy Seat and its cherubim at the two ends.

First, one must understand that the place in the sepulcher "where the body of Jesus had lain" before His resurrection, typifies the flat area (top) of the Mercy Seat. The two angels typify the two cherubim, "one at the head ...where the body of Jesus had lain" and "the other at the feet where the body of Jesus had lain."

As the two cherubim are one with "the two ends" of the Mercy Seat on the Ark built by Moses, so also the two angels are associated with the head and feet of Jesus, who is our Mercy Seat. One might say, "I hear what you are saying; however, how does the "sepulcher" — the place associated with the dead — relate to the entire Ark with its Mercy Seat?"

The Hebrew word for the **"ark"** used in the tabernacle of **Moses** is also translated as **"coffin"** in the Bible (Genesis 50:26). Yes, Joseph in the book of Genesis was buried in an ark (coffin); and he was one of those who was resurrected in Matthew 27:51-53. Thus, it is not

47

strange that it was in the "sepulcher" that the pattern of the Mercy Seat with its cherubim is also displayed; and this pattern is linked to the resurrection of Jesus.

The place of death has no power over the King of life (Remember, it was at the place "where the body of Jesus had (past tense) lain" were "two angels...sitting."). As indicated earlier, one angel (cherub) was at the end where the head of Jesus (Jesus' mind to show mercy) had lain, and the other angel was at the end where Jesus' feet (Jesus' judgment **with _and_ without** mercy) had laid.

1Corinthians 15:25: for he must reign, till he hath put all enemies under his feet.

*Revelation 1:13-15: 13And in the midst of the seven candlesticks one like unto the Son of man, clothed with a garment down to the foot, and **belted** about the **breast** with a golden **belt**. 14His head and his hairs were white like wool, as white as snow; and his eyes were as a flame of fire; 15 And **his feet like unto fine brass,** as if they burned in a furnace; and his voice as the sound of many waters.*

The Bible says that Jesus is the Head of the Church, and the Church is His body (feet) (Colossians 1:18). The "feet like fine brass" in Revelation 1:15 cited above represent "prayers" and "judgments" (the end of mercy as we know it for some in the Church and some outside the house of God). **"Brass"** is a compound of two Greek words, which is literally **"brass incense tree."** Brass is a symbol of judgment—think of the Brazen (brass) Altar in the Old Testament where the sacrifices were burned to God. Or think of the brazen serpent (a type of Jesus) in the book of Numbers (Numbers 21; John 3:14).

Incense is prayer according to Revelation 5:8 and Psalm 141. Thus, these cherubim at the two ends are a symbol of those who will preach Jesus as the Head of all, i.e., the head of the Church, the Head of principalities and powers, the Head of the kingdoms of men, and so on. "They shall prophesy" that Jesus' mercy, as we know it, shall come to an end! They will do this through the Spirit of prophesy and sackcloth—prayerful relationship with Jesus. They will also be witnesses of Jesus' resurrection power by the Spirit of intercession and fasting, typified by the sackcloth.

Saying it again, these angels (cherubim) are a symbol of those who preach Jesus and His resurrection (Luke 24:4; 24:6). You can tell false angels (pseudo messengers, pseudo preachers)! They do not preach Jesus; and if they do preach "a Jesus," they preach "another Jesus" which is according to men (2 Corinthians 11:4; Galatians 1). However, the two witnesses will declare **"the prophecy."** Jesus "in" His two cherubim will also tell His Church to stop weeping; Jesus is indeed alive (John 20:13-19)! We do not serve a dead God. Jesus declared that God is not the God of the dead. All live by Him, through Him and unto Him. Jesus is alive with real "flesh and bones;" and there is resurrection in Him.

He is the resurrection! Jesus is alive! Jesus is alive! Jesus is alive! The cherubim (angels) will declare this truth from the two ends of the Ark. They will declare the mind of Jesus (the one at the head). They will also preach the end of mercy as we know it (the feet of brass).

Yet, there is still a debate in the Church as to when the end of Jesus' mercy will be. When is the time that the Church will execute the judgments written (Psalms 149)? How can we know when it is the end of mercy? Is the Mercy Seat really Jesus and His Body as one Spirit? Who do the two Cherubim really represent? How do they relate to the tomorrow (the next 1,000 years)? Let us look again at Exodus 25:18-20 cited at the beginning of this chapter.

Exodus 25:18-20: *[18]And you shall make* **two cherubim** *of gold of beaten work shall you make them, in the* **two ends of the mercy seat.** *[19]And make one cherub on the one end, and the other cherub on the other end: even of the mercy seat shall you make the cherubim on the two ends thereof. [20]And the cherubim shall stretch forth their wings on high, covering the mercy seat with their wings, and their faces shall look one to another; toward the mercy seat shall the faces of the cherubim be.*

49

I remember reading the verses cited above some years ago. As I read, I heard words in the spirit of my mind say, *"there is an end to mercy!"* My spirit leaped as the Spirit of the Lord began to expound to me a meaning of the verses above. The instruction continued as He made plain to me that the cherubim were placed at the two ends of the mercy seat to typify that there will be "two ends" to the mercy of Jesus; and the cherubim are indeed the end of mercy.

One end may be at the end of this age when the Lord comes during the seventh or last trumpet to take His great power of resurrection and reign. The other end may culminate at the end of the day of the Lord (the seventh millennium), when He comes in His Glory and all His holy angels administer what appears to be the eternal judgment.

The cherubim at the two ends of the mercy seat also point to the two witnesses who will end mercy towards the world as we know it. The two prophets (the two witnesses) will smite the earth and smite those who "hurt" the two witnesses with all manner of plagues as often as they will, before and/or during the seventh (last) trumpet. Two or three witnesses must establish every word. Jesus is the first of the three witnesses. The two witnesses are the second and third of the three witnesses.

Exodus 25:18: And you shall make two cherubim of gold of beaten work shall you make them, in **the two ends of the mercy seat.**

Hebrews 9:3-5: [3]And after the second veil, the tabernacle which is called the Holiest of all; [4]which had the golden censer, and the ark of the covenant ...[5]And over it the cherubim of glory shadowing the **Mercy Seat (or propitiation) ....**

Romans 3:23-25: [23]For all have sinned and come short of the glory of God; [24] Being justified freely by his grace through the redemption that is in Christ Jesus: [25]Whom God hath set forth to be a **propitiation (or Mercy Seat)** *through faith in his blood ....*

1 John 4:10: Herein is love, not that we loved God, but that he loved us, and sent his Son to be the **propitiation (Mercy Seat)** *for our sins.*

Jesus is the Mercy Seat, as also indicated earlier in this chapter! The word **"propitiation"** used in Romans 3:24 is the same Greek word translated as **"Mercy Seat"** in Hebrews 9:5. Jesus is our Mercy Seat; and this Mercy Seat has two cherubim joined to Him.

As Jesus is the living Mercy Seat, so the two cherubs on the Mercy Seat also represent the two witnesses. This also makes the cherubim "persons" who are attached to Jesus. Thus, when Moses made the Mercy Seat and the cherubim all of one piece it points to the Person (Jesus) and His two witnesses. These two witnesses also include His Churches who are filled with golden olive oil (the Holy Spirit).

*Revelation 11:3-4: ³And I will give power unto **my two witnesses,** and they shall prophesy a thousand two hundred and threescore days, clothed in sackcloth. ⁴These are the two olive trees, and the two candlesticks standing before the God of the earth.*

*1 Kings 6:23: And within the oracle he made **two cherubim** of olive tree, each ten cubits high.*

As briefly discussed earlier, the two witnesses are representative of the two cherubim. The **"two witnesses"** are called **"two olive trees."** In Solomon's temple, the two cherubim of the Holy of Holies ("the Oracle") were also made of **"olive trees."**

Thus, a similarity can be drawn between the two witnesses (two olive trees) in Revelation 11 and the cherubim of olive trees in the temple built by Solomon. With that said, the Mercy Seat (which is one with the cherubim) was designed to remain in the Holy of Holies.

We learned earlier that the Holy of Holies of the tabernacle built by Moses (10 x 10 x 10=1,000 cubits (years)) is a pattern of a timetable that represents the millennium rule of **"the Christ"** and His saints **with** Him (Revelation 20:4-5). Thus, these cherubim's functions also relate to tomorrow the next 1,000 years. That is, they relate to the Holy of Holies (1,000 cubits), the inner temple. They relate to the two witnesses who are in the "measure" of the "temple of God...."

*Revelation 11:1: and there was given me a reed like unto a rod: and the angel stood, saying, Rise, and measure **the temple of God, and the altar,** and them that worship therein.*

First, John measured the temple of God as seen above. Second, he mentioned the authorization of the two witnesses to prophesy in Revelation 11:3. They are included in the measure of the temple and the altar. This temple of God with the associated altar is more than likely the temple of the Most Holy Place.

*Revelation 11:19: And **the temple of God** was opened in heaven, and there was **seen in his temple the ark** of his testament....*

Again, in the "temple of God" was "the ark," and "the altar" was also mentioned[20]. This is the Altar of Incense that was placed just outside the veil of the Holy of Holies which was at the end of the Holy Place, 2,000 cubits or years (Exodus 30:1 w/30:6).

The fact that it is placed at the end of the Holy Place going towards the Holy of Holies, demonstrates that the altar of incense is placed at the end of the current two thousand years Church age and/or just before the beginning of the one thousand years reign of "the Christ" and those who reign <u>with</u> Christ (those resurrected and/or translated in the first resurrection). It is also believed that this Altar of Incense was also placed just inside the Holy of Holies once a year.

*Hebrews 9:3-4: [3]And after the second veil, the tabernacle which is called the Holiest of all; [4]Which had the **golden censer (lit., "a vessel for burning incense, altar of incense),** and the ark of the covenant overlaid roundabout with gold....*

The Scriptures above indicate that there was "after the second veil...**the golden 'altar of incense.'"** The fact that John included the "altar" in the measure of the "temple of God" showed what era was

---

[20] I am also aware that the "temple of God" could include the Holy Place and the Most Holy Place (Ephesians 2:22; 1 Corinthians 3:16) which could then indicate that this "altar" could be the place of sacrifice (Revelation 6:9) <u>in lieu</u> of its being the place of incense (Revelation 8:3-5).

being signified. John measured the temple of the Holy of Holies (10 x 10 x 10=1,000 cubits (years).

As indicated above, the 1,000 cubits point to the 1,000 years reign of "the Christ" and those who reign <u>with</u> Him, and the altar of incense was included in the Most Holy Place. Again, for emphasis, Hebrews states that there was **"after** the second …called the Holiest of all…**the golden censor (or the golden altar of incense)."**

The measure of the Holiest of all (the Holy of Holies) is 1,000 cubits of years. Thus, the altar having been placed just inside the veil shows that this event takes place just before the "millennium" starts, or it is an indication that the next millennium age is about to come into effect.

The "action" (prophecies, judgments) of the two witnesses will also come into focus with respect to the same measurement of the temple and placement of the altar. Remember, according to Revelation 11:19, "the ark" was also seen in the temple of God. On this ark are the two cherubim. So, how do the two cherubim at the two ends of the mercy seat relate to the "action" of the two witnesses?

We learned earlier that the Mercy Seat is the Person of Jesus (Hebrews 9:5, Romans 3:25). The Altar is also a symbol of a person or persons. The Altar is Jesus as our Intercessor, the Holy Spirit as our Intercessor, and those who are intercessors in the Church in general.[21] It follows that the temple of God is also Jesus' people. Peter stated that we are a **"spiritual house"** made of **"living** stones" (1 Peter 2:5). Paul called the Church the temple of God.

*1 Corinthians 3:16: Know you not that **you are the temple of God,** and that the Spirit of God dwells in you?*

*Revelation 11:1: … the angel stood, saying, Rise, and measure the **temple of God, and the altar,** and them that worship therein*

---

[21] Hebrews 7:25; Rom 8:27; Rom 8:34

Revelation 11:19: And **the temple of God** *was opened in heaven, and there was seen in his temple the ark of his testament....*

John 2:19-21: [19]*Jesus answered and said unto them,* **Destroy this temple, and in three days I will raise it up.** [20]*Then said the Jews, Forty and six years was this temple in building, and will you rear it up in three days?* [21]*But* **he spoke of the temple of his body.**

As can be seen, the temple of God is the body of Jesus Himself, and His Body of believers. Thus, the fabricated buildings of Solomon and Moses point to living entities (Jesus and His Church). The fact that the two witnesses were mentioned in the context of the "temple of God" and "the altar" being measured represents the two cherubim in the "Oracle" of Solomon's Temple made of olive trees.

These two cherubim (or two witnesses) are consummate witnesses of God related to the resurrection of Jesus Christ. Their witness will range from giving the prophetic testimony of Jesus and His resurrection, to "mournfully"[22] tormenting the earth under God's authority by prophecy, fire, and plague. Their witness will culminate in their being raised from the dead as two witnesses of the resurrection power of the Spirit of holiness.

So let us review this again (Philippians 3:1). What does it mean to **"measure"** God's Body of believers ("the temple of God") with respect to the "end of mercy?" The temple of God in the tabernacle built by Moses is measured at 1,000 cubits (years). This "temple of God" represents Jesus and His body of believers who live in the Holy of Holies.

It also represents the 1,000-year rule of the resurrected and translated saints in the first resurrection. These first-fruit Christ and those who partake of the first resurrection (including the first to rise in His coming) will rule as kings and as priests with Christ. Again, according to Revelation, this rule will be for a thousand years before

---

[22] This is typified by the two witnesses being clothed in sackcloth.

54

the other resurrection at His coming where He will sit upon His Throne of Glory to administer eternal judgment.

The temple of God is also the place of the Altar of Incense (once a year) and the place of the Ark with the Mercy Seat and its two cherubim. These two cherubim are symbols of the two witnesses that the Apostle John included in the "measure" of the temple of God, the measure of the altar and the measure of the "worshippers."

Therefore, God is saying to the **apostles of this age** to measure the Church and prepare her for the day of the Lord (the next one thousand years of Christ's rulership). They are to measure the Temple of God with the understanding that "in" this rule (this measure) of the temple of God are also the living entities called the two witnesses.

They are as the two living cherubim who cover the Ark at the two ends of the Mercy Seat. They also represent the end of mercy for some. Yet, they function out of a life of prayer, intercession and mourning for the sins of those in the earth who do not believe in Jesus.

*Revelation 11:19: And the **temple of God** was **opened** in heaven, and there was seen in his temple the **ark** of his testament....*

*2 Chronicles 5:7-8: ⁷And the priests brought in the **ark of the covenant** of the LORD unto his place, to the oracle of the house, into the most holy place, even **under the wings of the cherubim:** ⁸For the cherubim spread forth their wings over the place of the ark, and the cherubim covered the ark and the staves thereof above.*

*1 Chronicles 28:11: Then David gave to Solomon his son the pattern of the porch, and of the houses thereof, and of the treasuries thereof, and of the upper chambers thereof, and of the inner parlors thereof, and of the place of the **mercy seat.***

*Exodus 25:18: And you shall make two cherubim of gold of beaten work shall you make them, in the **two ends of the mercy seat.***

*James 2:13: for he shall have **judgment without mercy,** that hath showed no mercy; and **mercy rejoices against judgment.***

As the cherubim represent the ends of the seat of mercy, so the two witnesses represent "judgments without mercy"[23] at the end of the Church age as we know it. **However, this "judgment without mercy" is also qualified to be <u>towards</u> those who "hurt" the two witnesses "unjustly."** If this is understood, then one will be able to understand why the two witnesses (two olive trees and two lampstands (Churches)) are identified as releasing fire that "devourers;" and a reason they are also called "hurtful ones." Saying it another way, men of God in this age will not be pushed around by the beast and its followers. These two witnesses will only allow themselves to be martyred by the beast when their time of witness is finished (Revelation 11:7).

As the temple of God is Jesus and the living body of believers; and as the Altar of Incense also represents Jesus and His intercessors; so, the two cherubim represent living people associated with the ends of the Mercy. This Mercy seat is Jesus. Jesus is "one" with the two ends of the Mercy Seat, being joined to His two witnesses through the Holy Spirit. Again, this is demonstrated by the cherubs that Moses built. They were one with the Mercy Seat. The measure of the temple of God which included the cherubim (the two witnesses) shows that the "two ends" of the Mercy Seat are now in the measure. That is, the beginning of the two ends of mercy has begun at the end of this age and will continue into the next age. The two witnesses will "smite the earth with **all plagues** as **often as they will**" (Revelation 11:6).

Note: I can teach this from the standpoint of the cherubim looking toward the blood on the mercy seat, looking toward the house of God, looking toward the **"end of the Lord" which "is mercy,"** and that **"mercy rejoices against Judgment."** These references to "mercy" are all true for the Church age and these truths also directly govern those who are qualified to be part of the two witnesses. However, the completing of this age is now speedily approaching. The two witnesses will come into their prophetic witness. It is to the faces of

---

[23] For those who are self-sent prophets, please do not use this statement to condemn the just or people in general.

56

each other they will look or "towards the house" of God that these witnesses will look to.

They will not "look at" or "look to" the faces of those who desire to hurt them, nor look to the faces of those whom God has commanded them not to look towards. I know this is strong. Yet, the same God who is a God of mercy is the same God who is a God of wrath against those who do not believe His Son (John 3:36). God, through His prophets makes serious choices sometimes (1 Samuel 16:7).

*Exodus 25:18-20: [19]And make one cherub on the **one end,** and the other cherub **on the other end:** even of the mercy seat shall you make the cherubim **on the two ends thereof.** [20]And the cherubim shall stretch forth their wings on high, covering the mercy seat with their wings, and their **faces shall look one to another.***

*2 Chronicles 3:13: The wings of these cherubim spread themselves forth twenty cubits: and they stood on their feet, and **their faces were inward (lit., towards (the) house).***

One of the meanings of the statement **"their faces shall look one to another"** is that they will be commanded not to look at the harsh end with the eyes of mercy. The two witnesses will only look towards the "house" of God, "the house which has the work of the cross in them." Ezekiel experienced this firsthand (Ezekiel 9:1 with Ezekiel 43:3).

The Lord had called for the seven men who had charge over the city. He told one of them to mark (seal with the cross) the ones who sigh and cry over all the abominations that were being committed in Jerusalem (Ezekiel 9:3-4 with Revelation 7:1-3). However, "to the others he said in mine hearing, go you after him through the city, and smite, **let not your eye spare,** neither have you pity (Ezekiel 9:5)."

Even though the prophet's heart was towards mercy for the people (Ezekiel 9:8), Ezekiel still had to destroy the city (Ezekiel 43:3). God Himself did the same as He had commanded the six "visitors" or "overseers" who had charge over the city: "And as for me [God] also, **mine eye shall not spare,** neither will I have pity, but I will recompense their way upon their head" (Ezekiel 9:10). These are strong statements. "It is a fearful thing to fall into the hands of the living God" (Hebrews 10:31).

As surely as there is full mercy in Jesus, there is an end of mercy for those who "obey not the gospel" (2 Thessalonians 1:8; 1 Peter 4:17). There will come a time that the earth will be reluctantly smitten will all manner of plagues by the two sons of fresh oil and the two candlesticks filled with the golden oil. (The two sons of fresh oil are those who constantly empty the golden oil into the witness of the two Churches.) It is difficult for me to make statements like this, yet even though my desire is for mercy; I am compelled to write these things.

The ends of mercy will come in the end of this age towards the next millennium. The two Churches will change their message and approach with respect to God's gospel. They will speak the message of "the prophecy." Yet, some kindred, tongues and nations will reject the testimony of Jesus.

 The message of the kingdom of God will be violently attacked; and God and the two lampstands (candlesticks) will return the favor. When the two prophets are treated hurtfully, they shall hurt the attackers with the same hurt for 1,260 days.[24] God will also terrify the great city with His "great power," the power of resurrection that will kill some famous names in Babylon.

*Revelation 11:5: And if any man will hurt them, **fire proceeds out of their mouth**, and devours their enemies: and **if any man will hurt them, he must in this manner be killed**.*

People of today have marginalized the judgments of God with love that rejoices in iniquity instead of love that "rejoices not in iniquity" (1 Corinthians 13:6). The two witnesses' judgments were so "devouring" and "hurtful" that they were called **"tormentors;"** and all the nations rejoiced when the witnesses were martyred.

---

[24] The 1,260 days is developed in *The Last Hour, the First Hour, The Forty-second Generation.*

This should not be strange that the Church will become confrontational. Did you know that Paul's witness turned the world upside down and his witness drove people out of their homes? Did you know that Paul so walked in the verdicts of God that they called him a "plague," "a protestor" and "one who causes uprising?"

*Acts 24:5: For we have found this man (Paul) a **pestilent** fellow, and a mover of sedition (stirrer of standing) among all the Jews throughout the world, and a **ringleader (lit., a protestor)** of the sect of the Nazarenes:*

*Revelation 11:10: And they that dwell upon the earth shall rejoice over them, and make merry, and shall send gifts one to another; because **these two prophets tormented** them that dwelt on the earth.*

Do not be deceived. The Lord will call for an end of mercy in the evening of this age. There will be plagues, pestilence, protests, and seditions against the three beasts, the sea, the earth, and so on (see the Book of Revelation). Will you have the "word of the Lord" to do what Jeremiah did in Jeremiah 28? Will you **"create"** what Moses did in Numbers 16:30?

Will you be **"filled with the Holy Spirit"** to do what Paul did in Acts 13? Will you be **"grieved"** to cast out other spirits of Python as in Acts 16? Are you willing to say what Peter "said" in Acts 8? Will you receive the gift of the **outpouring of the Holy Spirit** to "prophesy" as the two witnesses (two cherubs) in Revelation 11? The answer is yes!

Yes, if you believe that Jesus is the Christ, and your spirit confesses that Jesus Christ "is" come in the flesh! You will have the "gift" of the outpouring of the Spirit of prophecy to **mournfully** release His verdicts in the earth; **"if,"** and I repeat, "if" you belong to Christ, Jesus. It is God who "gives" unto His two witnesses to prophesy against the beast, spiritual Sodom, spiritual Egypt, nations, kingdoms, peoples, and tongues (Revelation 10 through Revelation 11; Revelation 17:15). There is "the day of vengeance of our God" that God's under-oarsmen or ministers will fulfill (Isaiah 61:2 with Luke 4:20).

*Revelation 11:3: **And I will give [power[25]] unto my two witnesses,** and they shall prophesy a thousand two hundred and threescore days, clothed in sackcloth.*

*1 Kings 6:27a: And **he set (lit., give) the cherubim** within the inner house....*

There is a prerequisite to this **"gift,"** you must be **"clothed in sackcloth"** (repentance, mourning and humility of soul with weeping, praying, and fasting — Psalms 30:11, Psalms 35:13; Matthew 11:21; Philippians 2:5-8; Daniel 9:3, Revelation 11:3). Saying it another way, you must be as the slain Lamb of God — that is you constantly lay down your life for the brothers/sisters (1 John 3:16, Revelation 5:9).

Saying it yet another way, you must be one who allows the God of Jesus to be the God of your spirit (Revelation 22:6, Romans 1:9, Luke 9:54-56). You must be of the seed of Jesus whose spirit confesses that Jesus Christ (our Mercy Seat) is come in the flesh (I John 2:2, 1 John 4:1-3). You must be one whose life (soul) is crucified with Christ and the life you now live you live by His faith (John 21:18, Galatians 2:20; Galatians 6:14; 17).

In other words, the cherubs at the two ends of the Mercy Seat were **"beaten work"** (Exodus 25:18). They were beaten into the two ends of the Mercy Seat to become one with the Mercy Seat. Therefore, they are one in/with the ends (plural) of the ages as briefly comprehended in 1 Corinthians 10:11. Thus, God will first "beat" the two witnesses into becoming merciful and interceding for mercy for all, including themselves. I believe this is why they were clothed in sackcloth. The purpose of becoming one with the Mercy Seat is that it must only take the "gifting" from God to end mercy for a short time (Revelation 11:1-13).

---

[25] This word "power" is cursive in the KJV and other versions because it was supplied by the translators and is not in the original texts. Thank the Lord for the translator's honesty.

The two witnesses will be so crucified with Christ that they will have to be "carried" (energized, gifted) by "another" (Spirit of Jesus) to execute the judgments written (see John 21:18). Paul was filled with the Holy Spirit to judge the sorcerer in Acts 13:9-11. **The "two witnesses" will execute the judgment written "without mercy" to those who reject "the Word of God," "the witness of Jesus," and to those who "showed no mercy."**

*James 2:13: for He shall have **judgment without mercy that** hath showed no mercy....*

In this age we live in, many of the less fortunate are being mercilessly abused by tyrants; in Africa, genocide; in the Middle East, war, and seditions; in some parts of South America, hideous drug killings; in other parts of the world, merciless women-mongering, and slave trading, and so on. Beastly mankind and antichrists will also **tread underfoot the Son of God;** they will reckon Jesus' blood as **"common;"** and **"spite" the Spirit of Grace.**

God will be "without mercy," He will "sorely punish" to "protect (the) honor" of His Son. And finally, God will show no mercy to beastly mankind who refuses to show mercy to the Church or to those who decline to show mercy to any who refuse the name of the beast, the number of his name, the mark of the beast and the number of the beast. Listen to the Holy Writ:

*Hebrews 10:28-29: [28]He that despised Moses' law died **without mercy** under two or three witnesses: [9]Of how much sorer **punishment (lit. to protect one's honor),** suppose ye, shall he be thought worthy, **who hath trodden underfoot the Son of God,** and hath counted the blood of the covenant, wherewith he was sanctified, **an unholy thing,** and hath done **despite** unto the Spirit of grace?*

*Revelation 13:11; 15: [11] And I beheld **another beast** coming up out of the earth; and... he had power to ... **cause that as many as would not worship the image of the beast should be killed.***

*James 2:13: for he shall have judgment **without mercy that** hath showed no mercy....*

Again, Why no mercy? Beastly mankind and antichrists will tread underfoot the Son of God; they will reckon Jesus' blood as "common;" and "outrage" the Spirit of Grace. That is, the beast and its followers will call the Holy Spirit an unclean spirit. Know this: Blasphemy against the Holy Spirit is the unpardonable sin.

God will eventually judge "without mercy," **He will "sorely punish" to "protect (the) honor" of His Holy Spirit, and the honor of the Son of His love.** And finally, after God's longsuffering comes to an end, He will show no mercy to beastly mankind because they refuse to show mercy to the Church or anyone who did not worship the beast, who did not receive the name of the beast, the number of his name, the mark of the beast and the number of the beast.

I implore you: Give your life to Jesus, now! He came and died for all our sin. He was resurrected for our justification. He will not remember your sins once you ask Him forgiveness.

Answer the urging of the Father who draws you to His Son, Jesus that you may be included in the measure of those who worship in the temple of God; because those who are outside His temple will be trampled. "But the court which is **without (outside)** the temple leave out and measure it not; for it is given unto the Gentiles: and the holy city shall **they tread under foot** forty and two months" (Revelation 11:2). It is time for action, give your life to Jesus, He is the Mercy Seat, our Propitiation.

TIME FOR "ACTION"

2 Chronicles 3:8: And he made the most holy house, the length whereof was according to the breadth of the house, twenty cubits, and the breadth thereof twenty cubits....

*2 Chronicles 3:10-11: ¹⁰And in the most holy house he made two cherubim of **image work (lit., sculptured (for) action),** and overlaid them with gold. ¹¹And the wings of the cherubim were twenty cubits long ....*

*1 Kings 6:23: And **within the oracle** he made two cherubim of olive tree, each **ten cubits high.***

Jesus indicated that the works that He did testify that He was indeed sent from the Father (John 5:36; John 10:25). The Church of Jesus must also show some **"action,"** as Jesus worked (John 5:20; John 14:12). The two cherubim give us a glimpse into this work or action that has to be performed through the Church of Jesus. There will be a time for action of the witnesses of the two candlesticks, or the two olive trees and the two prophets. This can be seen in the verses above.

I remember being a little perplexed with the verses above relative to the time for the "action" of the two cherubim in the "Tabernacle of the Set Time," built by Moses, and relative to the two witnesses in the book of Revelation. As discussed in the previous chapter, the two witnesses were "gifted" into "action" as John measured the temple of God, the altar, and the worshippers. This "measure" I understand to point to the beginning of the next 1,000-year rule of some of the saints with Christ; and/or, it may point to the end of the Church age as we know it.

This can be seen in the fact that the "altar" of incense was mentioned in the "measure" of the temple God. It is probably not the Brazen Altar because the place of the Brazen Altar "the court which is outside" the temple (the outer court) is not included in the measure (Revelation 11:2). With that said, the "altar" has to be the "Altar of Incense" (compare Rev 8). The Altar of Incense is usually placed at the end of the Holy Place (20 x10 x 10=2,000 cubits (years)).

That is, the Altar of Incense was placed at the end of the current Church age (2,000 years from Jesus Christ's death, burial, and powerful resurrection). In addition, we also learned that the Altar of Incense was placed in the Holy of Holies, just inside the veil, once a year (Leviticus 16; Hebrews 9). This indicates to me that the "action" of the two witnesses is indeed associated with the beginning of the millennium to come and the end of the current Church age. How?

They were mentioned in the "measure" of "the temple of God." This measure of "the temple of God" includes either both the Holy Place (2,000 years) and the Holy of Holies (1,000 years), or just the Holy of Holies alone. Let us look at it from the Holy of Holies. In the Holy of Holies is the placement of the Mercy Seat with the two cherubim (the two witnesses).

The Altar of Incense is also placed in the Holy of Holies once a year. Therefore, the two witnesses have "action" in the Church age and in the "age to come," since "the temple of God" (Holy of Holies) with all its furniture (Ark and Altar) are included in the measure. This truth is also illustrated in the temple built by Solomon.

The measure of the Holy of Holies (8,000 cubits) built by Solomon did not originally appear to relate to the times of action of the two witnesses as outlined in Revelation 11:1-14, nor did it appear to relate to the Holy of Holies of 1,000 cubits patterned by Moses. In the Tabernacle built by Moses, the cherubim on the Mercy Seat fell within the Holy of Holies.

Thus, I knew that they related to the Day of the Lord as defined by Peter to be 1,000 years. It was after much musing on the Scriptures that I was later taught by the Holy Spirit that the witness ("action") of the olive trees is also true for the temple built by Solomon.

The cherubim are components of both Holies of Holies (Moses' and Solomon's). Except that the calculated volume of the Holy of Holies for the "Tabernacle of Set Time" as built by Moses was 1,000 cubits of years. This fits beautifully with the duration of the Day of the Lord (1,000 years) as indicated previously.

However, Solomon's volume of 8,000 cubits (20 x 20 x 20) did not appear to relate to the duration of the Day (1,000 years) of the Lord to come. There appears to be a contradiction between Solomon's pattern and Moses' pattern. However, as I began to meditate on the placement of these "cherubim of action" and their measurements, the Spirit of Jesus began to show me the "action" of the two witnesses in the current age and the age to come.

He opened my understanding by showing me how the time of action of the two witnesses relates to measurements in Solomon's temple. The time of action of the two cherubs can be seen in the measurement from the doors of the Holy of Holies in Solomon's temple to the two standing cherubim and the Ark.

The Lord used the placement of the Ark, the two sculptured cherubim and the measurement of the Holy of Holies to outline times and seasons. With that said, it is not my intent to discuss in this Chapter everything piece by piece (Hebrews 9:5b).

My intent is to use the Scriptures to show that the two cherubim (two witnesses) are **"sculptured for action"** towards the end of the current 2,000 years of the Church age as we know it. Now, before I discuss the measure of time relative to the cherubim and the Ark, allow me to show another connection between the two witnesses of Revelation and the cherubim of the Holy of Holies for clarity.

Again, these two cherubim are symbols of the two witnesses in the book of Revelation. If you can receive this, the cherubim in Solomon's temple and the two witnesses are both called olive trees. There are two cherubim built in Solomon's days for Solomon's Holy of Holies.

There are also two witnesses. Both the two witnesses and the two cherubim are called "two olive trees" as seen in Revelation and 1 Kings (see references below). Olive trees also represent the golden olive oil that was poured into the candlesticks for prophetic action in their times.

*1 Kings 6:23: And within the oracle he made **two cherubim** of **olive tree**, each ten cubits high.*

*Revelations 11:3-4: ³And I will give power unto my **two witnesses**... ⁴These **are the two olive trees,** and the two candlesticks standing before the God of the earth.*

As can be seen above, both the cherubim and the two witnesses are called olive trees and are made from olive trees. The two witnesses are also called "lampstands" or "candlesticks," depending on which Bible version you prefer. According to Jesus, the "lampstands" are symbols of His Churches (Revelation 1:20). The fact that the two witnesses are called "olive trees" is significant because the Church made up of Jews and Gentiles is also called an olive tree, by Apostle Paul.

The Gentiles are called a "wild olive tree" and the Church made up of Jews and Gentiles is called "the olive tree." Why is this so important? The Church is also part of the "two witnesses" who shall judge the world; and out of the Church, the witnesses of the two sons of fresh oil are being sculptured for action. This should be a rebuke for those who feel they can do God's work apart from His Church as some are lone rangers. Every man of God needs the Body of Christ, and the Body of believers needs men of God. Nonetheless, the Church is part of the two witnesses.

*Revelation 11:3-4: ³And I will give power unto my two witnesses... ⁴These are the two olive trees, and the **two candlesticks** standing before the God of the earth.*

*Revelation 1:20: the mystery of the seven stars which you saw in my right hand, and the seven golden candlesticks. **The ... seven candlesticks which you saw are the seven churches.***

*Romans 11:17: And if some of the branches be broken off, and thou, being **a wild olive tree,** wert grafted in among them, and with them partakes of the root and fatness of **the olive tree.***

Jesus defines the Church as a "candlestick." Paul defines the same Church as "the olive tree." The two witnesses are two prophets. The two witnesses are also two Churches because "candlesticks" are defined as "Churches." The two witnesses are also two olive trees. They are also called the "sons of fresh oil" who "empty the golden oil out of themselves" into the Churches (Zechariah 4; Revelation 11). If the above made sense to you and you can continue on, let us now look at the measures in Solomon's temple.

First, one must understand that the Church can technically function in the Holy of Holies ("the age to come" or the 1,000 years rule or the Day of the Lord), now! The Church does not have to live in the Holy Place or the Outer Court. Even though we are indeed living through the period of the Holy Place (the current 2,000 years), it can be argued that this 2,000 years period was in the Holy of Holies, according to Solomon's temple.

In other words, just like Moses, Joshua, Daniel, Ezekiel, Jeremiah, Samuel, David, Jesus, and so on transcended the age they lived in to live in the Holy of Holies, so can the Church of Jesus Christ. The Church, the "Elect Lady" can function and is to function in the Holy of Holies without delaying in the other two chambers. This is done through the blood of Jesus.

*Hebrews 10:19: Having therefore, brethren, boldness to enter into **the holiest** by the **blood of Jesus**.*

The verse above is an invitation to pass the Outer Court mentally or in spirit. We can enter into the "holiest by the blood of Jesus." What a truth! Technically, there are not three chambers for those who have their conscience "pruned" by the blood of Jesus. There is only one room for the Church that was washed by the blood of Jesus.

We can live in that place of God's holy dwelling because of Jesus. The same is true with the two cherubim (the two witnesses) in the Holy of Holies in Solomon's temple. They are also a function of the Church age dwelling in the Holy of Holies. In other words, not only will the two witnesses be a function of the end of this age and the beginning of the Day of the Lord (1,000 years to come), but the two witnesses are also a function of the present age.

*2 Chronicles 3:10: And in the **most holy house** he made **two cherubim** of image work and overlaid them with gold.*

"The most holy house" was the place of the two cherubim. Thus, their measures and placement are within the confines of the Holy of Holies. Saying it another way, their function relative to the "Church age" (2,000 years) can also be ascertained from the two cherubim standing in the Holy of Holies. Or the proof that the two witnesses (the two olive trees) of the Book of Revelation relate to the current Church age, and the age to come is shown in the Holy of Holies of Solomon's temple. Let us look at some of the dimensions.

*1 Kings 6:27: And he set the cherubim within **(Hebrew: b^{a}towk, lit., in the middle of)** the inner house: and they stretched forth the wings of the cherubim, so that the wing of the one touched the one wall, and the wing of the other cherub touched the other wall; and their wings touched one another in the **midst (middle, Heb: towk)** of the house.*

The Cherubim were placed **"in the middle of the inner house."** This is significant to understanding the "action" of the two witnesses relative to the end of this age and the end of mercy. The length of the Holy of Holies is 20 cubits long (2 Chronicles 3:8). Thus, these two cherubim (two prophets) were 10 cubits back from the veil since they are placed "in the middle of the inner house." These cherubim's wings spread 20 cubits, the breadth of the Holy of Holies (2 Chronicles 3:11). The height of the cherubim were 10 cubits (1 Kings 6:23). Now let us put it all together.

The span of the two cherubim including theirs wings was 20 cubits. This measurement, multiplied by their heights of 10 cubits and multiplied by the distance to their location in the middle of the inner house (10 cubits from the veil) yields 2,000 cubits (years) — 10 x 20 x 10=2,000 cubits (years). If one looks at the entire measure of Solomon's temple, he/she will miss the "action" of the two cherubim (the two witnesses) for the Church age. The entire measurement of

Solomon's Holy of Holies (8,000 cubits) is linked to the coming of the Lord for eternal judgment "about [the] eighth day" and to inhabit His finished holy temple permanently in Spirit.

The two cherubs as a function of their height, width (including their wingspan) and location represent the approximate time that the two witnesses will take "action" with respect to the end of mercy, and/or the end of this age as we know it. This duration in which the two cherubs are taking "action" is to last approximately 2,000 years from Jesus Christ until their death, no burial and resurrection (2 Chronicles 3:10; Revelation 11). In addition, the dimensions also show that the two cherubim, the two witnesses, are being **"sculptured (for) action"** in the two thousand years. God has been wonderfully **"sculpturing"** the prophetic Church for the past 2,000 years for His **"action"** as defined in Revelation 11. What "action?" The "action" that will usher in the change of the ages!

The ages of the Church as we know it will come to an end. As surely as it is a historical fact that Jesus Christ came approximately 2,000 years ago, Daniel also saw a sure vision that **"the Ancient of Days came"** and **"time came"** for judgment to be given to the saints of the Most High (Daniel 7:21). Just like the Holy of Holies (1,000 cubits) is not seen until a person passes through "the veil." The Day of the Lord or the Day of Judgment (1,000 years according to Peter) will be seen after a "severe" experience at the end of this age. **"Veil"** literally means **"divider,"** according to Strong's' Concordance. **"Veil"** with its associated roots also literally means **severity, to break apart, rigor, cruelty.** Thus, severe cruelty will be experienced **"to break" from** the Church age, in order to usher in "the age to come" (compare Exodus 26:33).

As the age of the Law was changed to the ages of Jesus' Grace, so the ages of His Grace shall change to the "Day of God." There will not be the same kind of forbearance for some as we transition "into the age." Remember, the age of the law was ended severely by the crucifixion of Jesus. Remember, also that the age of the law was ended severely in A.D. 70.

Thus, the age of Jesus' Church was established. The King and His saints <u>with</u> Him shall judge the world to usher in the age to come (Ex.: Psalms 9:8, Psalms 96:13, Psalms 98:9, Daniel 7: 9-28, Zechariah 14:16-19, Acts 17:31, Romans 3:6, Genesis 18:25, Revelation 19:15, 1 Corinthians 6:2, Revelation 2:27, Jude 1: 14-15).

Remember the cherubim in the Tabernacle built by Moses were of **"beaten work"** (Exodus 25:18). The Hebrew root for these words also means **severity and harshness. As** indicated earlier, the root word for the "veil" of the Holy of Holies (the transition between the Holy Place (Church ages) and the Holy of Holies (1,000 years of the Lord's Day) also means **to fracture, break apart, severity, cruelty, rigor** (Exodus 30:6).

It will be harsh for the heathen in the evening of this age and in the age to come as the transition from this age into "that age" is introduced by severity. As indicated earlier, the Old Covenant (the age of the law) was taken away violently, to establish the current age of grace, according to the book of Hebrews.

Jesus was violently crucified to establish the second covenant; and because Jerusalem "below" rejected the Messiah, it was violently[26] removed in A.D. 70 to give way to the Jerusalem "from above" made of both Jews and Gentiles. It will be the same for "the age to come." In order to go past the veil of flesh (the veil of this age), there will be severe and violent dealings of God to take away the current age to establish the second. May the Lord continue to remember mercy in the day of His wrath! **"O LORD, I have heard your speech, and was afraid: O LORD,** revive your work in the midst of the years, in the midst of the years make known; **in wrath remember mercy** (Habakkuk 3:2).

---

[26] Note: this does not mean that this author is anti-Semitic or takes pleasure in the destruction of any Jew or a particular people. When my family came to America in 1975 from Jamaica West Indies, it was the Jews that took us in and showed kindness; and I still have Jewish friends. **Jesus** himself stated that Jerusalem would be destroyed in a violent way (Luke 19:41-44).

HOW LONG?

Daniel 12:4-6: 4But thou, O Daniel, shut up the words, and seal the book, even to the time of the end: many shall **rove about,**[27] *and knowledge shall be increased. 5Then I Daniel looked, and behold, there stood other two, the one on this side of the bank of the river, and the other on that side of the bank of the river. 6And one said to the man clothed in linen, which was upon the waters of the river, how long shall it be to the end of these wonders?*

Daniel 12:5-6, NKJ: 5Then I, Daniel, looked; and there stood two others, one on this riverbank and the other on that riverbank. 6And one said to the man clothed in linen, who was above the waters of the river, "How long shall the fulfillment of these wonders be?"

In Daniel 10:4, above, a picture of the Ark of the Covenant with its cherubim is seen again. The two cherubim are represented by the **"two others"** on each of the **"riverbanks."** "The Lord God of Israel" who communes with us from between the two cherubs is exemplified by the "man" clothed in linen.

This "united man,"[28] clothed in linen, (Jesus and those "united" "equally" with Jesus) was in between the "two others" above the waters (plural) of the river. The Hebrew text indicates that these "other two" were facing inward (towards the river), looking at the man clothed in the linen, as the cherubim on the Ark look inward, facing God who dwells between the cherubim (2 Samuel 6:2).

Careful study of Daniel 12 will show that these "two others" are linked to the two ends of mercy. The word "others" literally means "hinder," "hind part," "last," "end" (Strong's OT: #309, #310, and #319). Thus, the **"two others"** can also be translated as the **"two ends."** The man clothed in linen asked Daniel to "seal the book even to the time of the end …." Relative to this chapter of Daniel (Daniel 12), there are two items that must be looked at to have a good handle

---

[27] Hebrew base also means to turn aside, swerve, fall away, to row, to whip or lash
[28] See my book *Vision Real* for further development.

on what the time of the end looks like. First one should ask: What are the indications of "the time of the end?"

Secondly, one should consider the duration, **"how long** shall it be to the end …?"** In addition, one must understand that there are those who "really" can tell the indications of the end and "how long" until the end (Psalms 74:9[29]), and the man clothed in righteousness (linen) gave the answers to both questions.

During the time of the end, there will be many who travel extensively **(rove about or run to and from).** In this age, the duration of travel from place to place is shortened, thus people travel to "far" lands frequently. In addition, the phrase **run to and from or rove about is used of the "eyes of the Lord;"** used of those who seek God's Word and cannot find answers, used of mariners, of rowers, of those who take unlawful censuses of Church membership, and so on. In other word, there appears to be multiple application the phrase "rove about" (Numbers 11:8; 2 Samuel 24:2; 2 Samuel 24:8; 2 Chronicles 16:9; Job 1:7; Jeremiah 5:1; Jeremiah 49:3; Ezekiel 27:8; Ezekiel 27:26; Amos 8:12; Zechariah 4:10).

During the time of the end, **"knowledge (lit., the knowledge) shall be increased."** The phrase "the knowledge (hadaa`at)" is used approximately five times in the Bible. It is used of "the knowledge of God" (Hosea 4:6 (twice); Jeremiah 22:16); it is used of "cunning to work (lit., the knowledge (of)) all work in brass" (1 Kings 7:14); and it is used of "the knowledge of good and evil" (Genesis 2:9; 17). One can see that in these days, "the knowledge" of God is increased. The knowledge of God that is currently being revealed by Jesus to His Church is so vast. These are things regarding Jesus that were hidden from most in previous generations that are now being revealed to His holy apostles and prophets. There is also "the knowledge" of the working of brass (understanding the depth of Jesus' crucifixion, as seen in the brazen altar and the brazen serpent; understanding the

---

[29] In Psalms 74:9, the "signs" are apostles (2 Cor 12:12). Those who "know how long" are the sons of Issachar (a type of Jesus who "paid the price" for us).

72

verdicts of God that are being executed through His worshipping Church, typified by Jesus' feet of brass in Revelation 1.) "The knowledge" to work metal has also improved significantly. Almost anything can be made from metal with precision these days.

"The knowledge" of good and evil is also increased. As the Church's knowledge of "the only God" increases more and more, so those who pursue evil are also increasing in the knowledge of the evil. Daniel's texts also give an answer as to "how long shall it be to the end ....?

*Daniel 12:7: And I heard **the man clothed in linen,** which was upon the waters of the river, when he held up his right hand and his left hand unto heaven and swore by him that lives **forever** that it shall be for **a time, times, and a half;** <u>and</u> **when he shall have accomplished to scatter the power of the holy people, all these things shall be finished.***

The "united man" (Jesus) in linen has the answers. First: The duration from Daniel's revelation to the time of the end is "time, times and a half."[30] The first step in understanding the Scripture is to see "what" has been said and "how" it is being said (Luke 10:26). Thus, definition becomes important as to the "how" a statement is being made. The words "time" and times" are also translated as "congregation" and "set time" in the Scriptures. The word "half" is regularly translated as "half" (חצי CHTZY) in the Bible and means "to cut or split in two" (Strong's OT: #2677, #2673). According to "Gesenius Hebrew-Chaldea Lexicon to the Old Testament" and other Hebrew lexicons the Hebrew word translated as "half" (חצי CHTZY) is also translated as "arrow" as in, an arrow that "divides" (1 Samuel 20:36-38, 2 Kings 9:24).

---

[30] Time, times, and half may mean 2,000 years; 4,000 years and 1,000 years (7,000 years total); or 3,500 years from when Daniel saw the vision, or 3 ½ years (1 year, 2 years and ½ a year); or 42 months; or 42 generations (~2,000 years); or one hour (42 years). See my book *The Last Hour, The First Hour, the Forty-second Generation.*

73

*1 Samuel 20:36: And he said unto his lad, Run, find out now the arrows (Hebrew: hachitsiym) which I shoot. And as the lad ran, he shot **an arrow (Hebrew: ha cheetsiy)** beyond him.*

*Daniel 12:7: And I heard the man clothed in linen, which was upon the waters of the river, when he held up his right hand and his left hand unto heaven and swore by him that lives **forever** that it shall be for a time, times, and a **half (Hebrew: cheetsiy)**....*

Now the clarifications above may seem strange without understanding. In 2 Kings and 1 Samuel, where the word for "half" is translated as "arrow," the arrow was used as a symbol of the separation of two houses (David being separated from Saul).

The arrow was also shot "a distance" "beyond" the lad. Thus, the arrow that was shot, can mean time continues "a distance" just beyond the "youth." The phrase "time, times and a half" can also read "congregation, congregations and an arrow (beyond)."

Time will continue "beyond" the set times of the congregations that are still a "youth." The congregations must mature past a child, past a young man, to become fathers in the earth (compare 1 John 2:12-14). The Lord tends to go just "beyond" man's predictions. God will allow the Goliath attitude to grow "a span" beyond six cubits (1 Samuel 17). God tends to go just beyond man's timetable. There is time, times, and a half time (arrow's shot beyond). Also, if you can receive it, the "half" may also symbolize the congregations that were separated by the "arrow" of separation. The house of David (a type of house of Jesus, the Beloved) will be separated from the house of Saul (house of Sheol) by the "arrow" of separation. This separation of the "congregations" can also be seen in Jeremiah.

*Jeremiah 24:1-2: [1]The LORD showed me, and behold, two baskets of figs were **set (Hebrew: mowʽᵃdiym, congregations)** before the temple of the LORD ... [2]One basket had **very good figs,** even like the figs that are first ripe: and the other basket had very **naughty figs,** which could not be eaten, they were so bad.*

There were two baskets of figs. One basket had first ripe figs (very good figs); and the second basket had very evil figs. So likewise, at the end (completion) of the age, there will be two congregations "set." The one congregation will consist of good saints, like "first-fruit" saints. These **"like"** the first-ripe are people whose "spirits confess Jesus" the same as their "mouths" confess Jesus.

The other congregation will be those who are bad (they live by sight). They do not "live by the faith of the Son of God." They cannot offer themselves as food to anyone in order to bring healing (contrast Revelation 22:2; Ezekiel 47:12). The congregation of the Lord is to bring forth good fruits that can be picked and eaten by others. Let us be "very good figs," "useful to our Master" (Jeremiah 24:2 with 2 Timothy 2:21).

There will also be a separation between those who "labor" for Christ an arrow shot "beyond" others as opposed to those who did not labor. There are those like Jesus who will allow God to throw them as a stone in prayer just "a little further" beyond others, even under the pressure of eminent death. "And He [Jesus] went a little further,[31] and fell on his face, and prayed, saying, O my Father, if it be possible, let this cup pass from me: nevertheless, not as I will, but as you will" (Matthew 26:39).

There are those in Christ who will "labor additional" to multiply their talents. In Luke 19:16, the servant with ten talents gained ten more talents because he "worked additionally." "Then came the first, saying, Lord, your pound hath gained (lit., worked additionally) ten pounds." This servant was distinguished from the other servant who just "produced" and from another servant who did not work to multiply. The servant who did not multiply the talent buried his talent.

There are those like Paul who will labor more than all the other apostles. "But by the grace of God I am what I am: and his grace

---

[31] Luke 22:41 (NAU) said that Jesus went "a stone's throw." This is the "stone" that crushed the image in Daniel 2.

which was bestowed upon me was not in vain; but I labored more abundantly than they all: yet not I, but the grace of God which was with me" (1 Corinthians 15:10). Others did indeed labor for the Lord Jesus. However, Paul labored a little more through the grace of God.

Finally, the united man clothed in linen also stated that the wonders would continue until the power of the holy people are not scattered anymore. Yes! The end will not come until the "power" that was imparted to the Church through the Holy Spirit is not shattered anymore. Christ in us, who is the power of God, must be demonstrated through His Church (1 Corinthians 1:24).

*Daniel 12:7: And I heard the man clothed in linen, which was upon the waters of the river, when he held up his right hand and his left hand unto heaven, and swore by him that lives forever that it shall be for **a time, times, and a half; and when he shall have accomplished (lit., finished)** to scatter the power of the holy people, all these things shall be finished.*

"These things shall be finished" when "the power of the holy people" is no longer being "scattered" or shattered. In other words, when the Church rises up and stops allowing its power (hand) to be scattered and uses its power (hand) as an instrument of righteousness, these things will be finished.

Saul's persecution was scattering David, but eventually Saul died, and David ruled. Saying it yet another way, some believe that "the beast" will be a power that cannot be matched. On the contrary, Jesus and His holy people will rise and use Jesus' power to overcome the beast (Revelation 17:14; Revelation 14; Revelation 19). Daniel overcame the beast and its system in his days. The apostles and saints overcame the fourth beast in their days. Many Christians have overcome the beast systems of our days.

With all that was said above, an angel in the book of Revelation stated something similar to the man clothed in linen in Daniel. The time, times and half duration finally came to the season when there will be **"time (Greek: chronos or uninterrupted time) no longer."**

Revelation 10:5-6: *⁵And the angel which I saw stand upon the sea and upon the earth lifted up his hand to heaven, ⁶And swore by him that lives forever and ever, who created heaven, and the things that therein are, and the earth, and the things that therein are, and the sea, and the things which are therein, that there should be* **time no longer.**

This angel stated, "that there should be time no longer."[32] One of the meanings of this is in respect to the mystery of the glory of "Christ in us" being released without delay. God through the mature saints will interrupt the normalcy of time. This is verified by Revelation 10:7. In the book of Daniel, the power of the holy people is being scattered and shattered until a "time."

That is, there is an apparent delay with regard to the release of power for deliverance to those who need the "ability of the Spirit." However, there is an "immediate … way of the Lord." Yet, the Scriptures reveal that mature sons of the devil can also affect the "immediate way of the Lord." However, the Scriptures also teach that the "rod" that God's mature "Son" rules with is the "rod of 'immediacy'" that overcomes any apparent delays.

In the days (plural) of seventh or last trumpet, there is no longer any "time" (delay) with respect to the glory of Christ being released in the earth. The mystery of Christ in us will finally be completed and finished. The power of the holy people will no longer be scattered or shattered. "All these things shall be finished."

Revelation 10:5-7: *⁵And the angel … swore by him that lives forever and ever …that there should be time no longer: ⁷But in the days of the voice of the seventh angel … the mystery of God should be* **finished** ….

Colossians 1:27: To whom God would make known what is the riches of the glory of **this mystery** *among the Gentiles, which is* **Christ in you, the hope of glory:**

---

[32] See also my book *The Days of the Seventh Angel* for more details.

THE TIME TRIBE

*Daniel 7:21-22: [21]I beheld, and the same horn made war with the saints, and prevailed against them; [22]Until the Ancient of days came, and judgment was given to the saints of the Most High; and **the time came** that the saints possessed the kingdom.*

Jesus Christ and His baptized believers, Abraham's seed, have been spoken of by the Father for 4,000 years before Jesus' first coming. It may have appeared that the words of His prophets were only speaking empty hope for those 4,000 years. However, **"the time came"** when Jesus, the Messiah did indeed come after that long duration of 4,000 years. It is an historical fact that He did indeed walk the land of Israel almost 2,000 years ago.

Well, for 2,000 years since Jesus' death, burial, and resurrection, it has been proclaimed that Jesus will come again. In fact, the Lord made the "promise" that He would come again; and as surely as He came the first time, He will come again! The saints have been suffering, for approximately 6,000 years, in various degrees depending on the hemisphere of their dwelling. And there will come a time when they reverse the abuse and rule the earth. "The **ancient of days came** and judgment was given to the saints of the Most High; and the time came that the saints possessed the kingdom."

For approximately 2,500 years sin was not reckoned by law (Romans 5:13-14). That era came to an end. Moses then brought in the age of law. The age ruled by legalism (law) also came to an end after 1,500 years by the sacrifice of Jesus. The age we now live in, which some have defined as the "Church age," will only last for approximately 2,000 years.

As surely as the age of no written law came to an end, and as the age of the Law instituted by Moses also came to an end, this age has an end. God told Abraham that the slavery of the children of Israel would end in 400 years. Even though God waited an additional 30 years, the Israelites' bondage came to an end. Thus, shall it be in the evening of this age; this age as we know it shall come to an end. "The time came …."

We have briefly looked at the time of His coming from many perspectives in the previous chapters. Now we will look at His coming from the standpoint of His tribes (Jew and Gentile believers). God obviously chose the Hebrew language and the Greek language in which to write His Scriptures. I conclude that the Holy Spirit must have been concerned about definitions relative to spiritual things. This does not mean that other languages are of no use, because the Bible is also translated into many languages.

What I am saying is that the Hebrew base word (מטה – MTH) reading from right to left) that is translated as **"came"** (MᵃTaaH) in its inflection, is the same Hebrew word translated as **tribe, rod, couch, bed,** and so on. Therefore, these words came out of the base word.

Jesus came out of God (God Fathered Him); and thus, He was **"equal"** with God (John 5:18). The words tribe, rod, came, couch all came out of the same base word. Thus, the meanings of these words are also in the base word and are "equal" to the base word. We call it etymology of words. For this writing I am only interested in the word "tribe."

The phrase **"the time came"** can be translated as **"the time tribe."** In other words, "time" is associated with Jesus' "tribes" according to its etymology. This "time tribe" is associated with the "Ancient of days." The **Ancient of days** is Jesus who was weaned from days and restored to eternal living.

There will be a "tribe" that will be just like Jesus. This "tribe" is that "perfect (corporate) man" mentioned in Ephesians 4:13. If you can receive it, the tribe will be "equal" to Jesus "in age" (spiritually); "as big as" Jesus in spiritual stature;[33] and "equal to Jesus by having the mind of Christ. This means that part of the requirement for when "the time came" is when there is a "tribe" in the earth that will be "equal" to Jesus' stature. Except, the Father, Jesus and the Holy Spirit still have the preeminence in all and overall.

Daniel 7:13: I saw in the night visions, and behold, one like the Son of man came with the clouds of heaven and **came to (or an equal tribe to)** *the* **Ancient of days (lit., Weaned from days),** *and they brought him near before him.*

John 5:18: Therefore, the Jews sought the more to kill him, because he not only had broken the Sabbath, **but said also that God was his Father,** *making himself* **equal** *with God.*

Ephesians 4:13: Till we all come in the unity of the faith, and of the knowledge of the Son of God, unto a perfect man, unto the measure of the **stature (lit., same age as)** *of the fullness of Christ:*

Jesus is **equal** with God because God is His Father (He was procreated by the Father). So likewise, we, who are born of God, have the potential to become **equal** with Jesus in this earth (1 John 5:1; Ephesians 4:13). In fact, Jesus said that those who are "perfect" (or fully equipped, mended) "shall be **as** his Master" (Jesus) (Luke 6:40; Matthew 10:25). We will do the same works that Jesus did in this earth, with a mature understanding of who we are as "sons" (Galatians 4:6-7).

"In the night visions" Daniel saw one "like the Son of man." He did not say this person was the Son of man. He said this person was "like" Him. That means this person can be Jesus, Himself, and this person can also be those who become like Jesus. Daniel also said that this person is "one like the Son of man ... and came to the Ancient of

---

[33] Stature in context of John 9:21 (among other meanings) can be understood to mean the ability of a person who is of age to speak or answer all about oneself relative to God's plan for that person just as Jesus was able to.

Days." As indicated earlier, this word **"came"** in Daniel 7:13 can also be translated as **"tribe."**

The two words **"and"** and **"to,"** used in Daniel 7:13, are translated from a Hebrew word **"`ad."** This word **"`ad."** is defined as: **"as far (or long, or much) as**, whether of space (even unto) or time (during, while, until) or **degree (equally with),"** witness (see Strong's Lexicon Old Testament #5704, #5705 and 5707).

Thus, Daniel 7:13 could read: "I saw in the night visions, and behold, one like the Son of man came with the clouds of heaven and came as an 'equal' tribe to the Ancient of days ...."

The one "like" the Son of man "came **'as an equal tribe'** to the Ancient of Days." As indicated earlier, this "Ancient of Days" is Jesus. The "one like the Son of man" can also point to the mature believers in the Church who are presented **"as equals"** to Jesus in the oneness of His faith and the oneness of His knowledge for rulership of the nations with Jesus.

"Ancient of Days" literally reads "Transferring of Days" or "Weaned of Days." The Hebrew word "attiyq" (at-teek') translated as "Ancient" is also used for babies that are drawn (weaned) from the breast and is defined as "weaned" by Strong's Concordance.

Isaiah 28:9: Whom shall he teach knowledge? And whom shall he make to understand doctrine? Them that are weaned from the milk and drawn ("attiyq" (at-teek') from the breasts.

For babies to be "weaned" from the breast, they had to have partaken of breast milk. For the "Ancient of Days" to be "weaned from days," He had to have lived in time. This is Jesus. He came from eternity and lived in time approximately 2,000 years ago. He then had to be "weaned" from the time realm and restored to His original glory, the glory of the "Ancient of Days."

Thus, Jesus is the One on the Throne who gave the kingdom of the earth to His mature believers — those who have become "like" Him or those who have become "as big as" Him. The goal of Christ for His

Church is for us to come to the same age as Him, which is to be weaned from days. We call it conquering the last enemy — death.

Ephesians 4:13: Till we all come in the unity of the faith, and of the knowledge of the Son of God, unto a perfect man, unto the measure of the **stature (lit., one of the same age, as big as, prime)** *of the fullness of Christ.*

The verse above also compliments Daniel 7:13 and Daniel 7:22. The Church is to come to the "measure of the 'same age' of the fullness of Christ." The saints are to become an "equal tribe" that will be "as big as" Him. Thus, one can conclude that "the time came" for the saints to possess the kingdom when the "time tribe" was equal in maturity to Jesus.

The Church has to grow up into the image of Jesus. It is not robbery to be equal with Jesus because we have been regenerated (re-gene) by the washing of water, and we "let" the same mind that was in Jesus mature in us (Philippians 2:5-6). There will be an equal tribe like Jesus in the earth. The more God's Word and the Holy Spirit renews our mind, the more we will realize that we have the gene of Jesus and the same mind of Jesus. Jesus is the Patriarch of us, His tribe!

Daniel 7:13: I saw in the night visions, and behold, one like the Son of man came with the clouds of heaven, and **came (or lit., an equal tribe)** *to the* **Ancient of days (lit., Weaned from days),** *and they brought him near before him.*

Daniel 7:22: until the Ancient of days came, and judgment was given to the saints of the most High; and the **time came (or time tribe)** *....*

The verses above with their definitions also show that "time" is associated with the "tribe" of Jesus (I mentioned this earlier). This was not a foreign concept to the early apostles. Paul and Peter taught similar things. Paul stated that the ends of the ages are "in" the saints. Peter stated that we "speed" the promised return of Jesus.

*1 Corinthians 10:11: Now all these things happened unto them for ensamples: and they are written for our **admonition, upon (lit., into) whom the ends of the world (lit., ages)** are come.*

*2 Peter 3:12: Looking for and **hasting unto (lit., speeding unto)** the coming of the day of God, wherein the heavens being on fire shall be dissolved, and the elements shall melt with fervent heat?*

Paul stated that the "ends of the ages" are come "into" the saints. That means that the "ends" are associated within the Church. It is in us, not outside of us that the ages will end. Peter also made a bold statement. The Church can **"speed** the coming of the day of God."

We learned that this "day of God" can point to the 1,000 years after the first resurrection. When Paul made his statement about the "ends of the ages" being "into" the saints it was in the context of saints living according to God. When Peter used the phrase of "'speed' the coming of the day of God," it was also in the context of the saints coming to "repentance."

There is a difference between forgiveness and repentance. Peter stated that the promise of His coming is "slowed" not because God is "slack." He is actually waiting for us. God is "longsuffering to us-ward, not willing that any should perish, but that all should come to repentance." Thus, Peter's statement later in which he said let us "speed" His coming.

*2 Peter 3:9: The Lord is not **slack** concerning his promise, as some men count slackness; but is longsuffering to us-ward, not willing that any should perish, but that all should come to **repentance.***

What Peter is conveying is that if we do not **repent**, then the promised coming will be delayed by "us." (2 Peter 3:4 with 2 Peter 3:9; 12). Repentance, by Greek definition, means to change one's mind. This is different from forgiveness, which means to send (one's sins) away. One of the purposes of forgiveness is to bring a person to **"change his/her mind."** Repentance is one of the things that will **"speed"** His coming. He does not want any of His followers to "perish." He wants all to repent—change their mind set.

Thus, when we change our mind set, we speed His coming. Saying it another way, Jesus will not come until the **"us-wards"** have repented to His satisfaction. The "ends of the ages" have come "into" us. When the Church repents, the "ends" that are already "in" us will be manifested, when He comes "in" His saints and finally when He comes "with" all His saints.

The end is also linked to the gospel of the kingdom being preached in all the occupied houses by believers. Thus, in this again, we see that time is linked to the Church. Apparently, the end cannot come until "then." The time came, then! When is "then?" When, the Church preaches the gospel of the kingdom in all the occupied houses as "a witness" unto all nations.

*Matthew 24:14: And this gospel of the kingdom shall be preached **in all the world for** a witness unto all nations; and then shall the end come.*

First, the verse above in the context of the entire chapter of Matthew 24 is linked to the destruction of Jerusalem in A.D. 70. In continuance, it can also apply to the "end" of this age and/or the end that will occur after Jesus' physical coming. Many may make predictions about the end of the ages. However, one of the pivotal factors is the gospel of the kingdom being preached **"in all the occupied houses."**

The phrase **"in all the world"** literally reads **"in all the occupied house."** The Greek word translated as "world" is "oikoumene;" and it is used for the inhabited world and means to "occupy a house." Thus, the "world' is the "the inhabited world" including "all" the "houses" that are "occupied" by people. The verse did not stop there. This gospel of the kingdom must also be "a witness," "a witness"[34] as God means it. It is not "a witness" as it is diluted to mean today. The Church has "additional work" and "greater works" to do. There are many Media to fulfill this word. There is writing, television, internet, radio, and so on. Oh! And do not forget the original way as

---

[34] Compare Revelation 11; I also recommend all Christians read Richard Wurmbrand's book, *Tortured for Christ.*

employed by Jesus and the early Church, "house to house" preaching of the gospel of the kingdom of God.

Also, as indicated earlier, the maturity of some is also linked to when "the time came." These mature ones are the "equal tribe" to Jesus. In other words, the **"time tribe"** that "came" is a tribe that is at the same "age" of Jesus when this tribe fully appropriates the blood of Jesus into repentance. Let me explain.

Daniel 7:13: I saw in the night visions, and behold, one like the Son of man came with the clouds of heaven, and **came to (or lit., an equal tribe to)** *the* **Ancient of days (lit., Weaned from days),** *and they brought him near before him.*

Daniel 7:22: until the Ancient of days came, and judgment was given to the saints of the most High; <u>and</u> *the* **time came (or time tribe)** *....*

Ephesians 4:13: Till we all come in the unity of the faith, and of the knowledge of the Son of God, unto a perfect man, unto the measure of the **stature (lit., one of the same age, as big as)** *of the fullness of Christ.*

The knowledge of the Son of God is unto "**a perfect man.**" This "perfect man" is also defined as the measure of the "stature (same age as)" the fullness of Christ. Perfection[35] according to the Scripture also includes <u>not</u> being conscious of sins.

Hebrews 10:1-2: [1]For the law having a shadow of good things to come ...can never with those sacrifices which they offered ... make the comers thereunto **perfect** *[2]... because that the worshippers once purged should have had* **no more conscience of sins.**

Hebrews 9:14: How much more shall the blood of Christ, who through the eternal Spirit offered Himself without spot to God, **purge (or pruned) your** *conscience from dead works to serve the living God?*

Hebrews 10:14: For by one offering He hath **perfected 'into the through-carried'** *them that are* **sanctified.**

---

[35] "Perfection" or "maturity," ultimately, is eternal life in glorified bodies.

One of the benefits of repentance is not to be conscious of sins as Christ was not conscious of any sins against Himself. Jesus had no sin even though He was tempted at all points; and He had to be made perfect in this area.

Christ's blood, through His sacrifice, has forever (into the age) "pruned" our conscience from sin; and purged us form the consciousness of sins. The "time tribe" that is an "equal tribe" with Jesus is the tribe that is **perfected (lit., matured)** from being conscious of sins. They have been made perfect through Jesus like Jesus was made perfect.

*Hebrews 5:8-9: [8]Though he was a Son yet learned He obedience by the things which he suffered; [9]And being made **perfect,** he became the author of eternal salvation unto all of them that obey him.*

*Hebrews 4:15: For we have not a high priest which cannot be touched with the feeling of our infirmities; but was in all points **tempted like as we are, yet without sin.***

Jesus was tempted like us; and if He had not known His Father He could have been conscious of these temptations. However, Jesus was "made perfect" in His conscience like we have to be, even though He was "in all points tempted like as we are, yet without sin."

He could have been tempted to believe that His temptation disqualified Him like humans tend to believe. However, He was matured in His conscience through His faith and obedient relationship with the Father. We likewise are perfected (matured) when we realize that the law is not our master anymore. "For the **law made nothing perfect (lit., mature)**" (Hebrews 7:19a). We are only perfected (not being conscious of any sins that Jesus has purged from us) through the one sacrifice of Jesus.

*Hebrews 10:1-2: [1]For the law having a shadow of good things to come, and not the very image of the things, can never with those sacrifices which they offered year by year continually make the comers thereunto **perfect.** [2]For then would they not have ceased to be offered? Because that the worshippers once purged should have had no more conscience of sins.*

*Hebrews 10:14: For by one offering He hath **perfected 'into the through-carried'** them that <u>are</u> **sanctified.***

*Hebrews 9:14: How much more shall the blood of Christ, who through the eternal Spirit offered Himself without spot to God, **purge (or prune) your conscience** from dead works to serve the living God?*

Why is this perfection of not being conscious of sins so important? Perfection is associated with Jesus Himself. Perfection is associated with showing mercy on the just and unjust; Perfection is associated with spirits of just men. Perfection is associated with resurrection life and power, and so on. Thus, the "tribe" that is "equal" with Jesus is the "first-fruits Christ" that will walk in everything that Jesus did in the earth. They will walk in His mercy. They will fellowship with His suffering and attain unto the resurrection out from among the dead (Philippians 3). We established earlier that "The Ancient of days" is the "Weaned of days." Thus, those who are perfected in conscience through the blood of Jesus are those who will be weaned from days. They will no longer be limited by time, in time. They will be weaned "into the age" with "endless life." They will be "like" the Son of man. The saints and the "time tribe" will possess the kingdom. "The time came;" and Jesus is "the only Potentate, the King of kings and Lord of lords!" Amen.

Prayer opportunity

If you are not currently sure if you will partake of the resurrection of the just ones, here is a prayer you can pray:

"I confess with my mouth the Lord Jesus; and I believe in my heart that God has raised Jesus from the dead. Because, with my heart I believe that Jesus is the Christ, the Son of the living God into righteousness, and with my mouth I make confession into the salvation Jesus has provided for me. Amen!" (See 1 John 5:1, Romans 10:9-10 and Ephesians 1:12-13 below).

1 John 5:1: Whosoever believeth that Jesus is the Christ is born of God.

Romans 10:9-10: [9]That if you shall confess with your mouth the Lord Jesus and shall believe in your heart that God hath raised him from the dead, you shall be saved. [10]For with the heart man believeth unto righteousness; and with the mouth confession is made unto salvation.

Ephesians 1:12-13: [12]That we should be to the praise of His glory, who first trusted in Christ. [13]In whom you also trusted, after that you heard the word of truth, the gospel of your salvation: in whom also after that you believed, you were sealed with that Holy Spirit of promise.

Other Books

Poiema, by Judith Peart
Wisdom from Above, by Judith Peart
Procreation, Understanding Sex, and Identity, by Judith Peart
100 Nevers, by Judith Peart
The Shattered and the Healing by Judith Peart
The Lamb, by Donald Peart
Jesus' Resurrection, Our Inheritance, by Donald Peart.
Sexuality, By Donald Peart
Forgiven 490 Times, by Donald Peart w/Judith Peart!
The Days of the Seventh Angel, By Donald Peart
The Torah (The Principle) of Giving, by Donald Peart
The Time Came, by Donald Peart
The Last Hour, the First Hour, the Forty-Second Generation, by Donald Peart
Vision Real, by Donald Peart
The False Prophet, Alias, Another Beast V1, by Donald Peart
"the beast," by Donald Peart
Son of Man Prophesy Against the false prophet, by Donald Peart
The Dragon's Tail, the Prophets who Teach Lies, by Donald Peart
The Work of Lawlessness Revealed, by Donald Peart
When the Lord Made the Tempter, by Donald Peart
Examining Doctrine, Volume 1, by Donald Peart
Exousia, Your God Given Authority, by Donald Peart
The Numbers of God, by Donald Peart
The Completions of the Ages … by Donald Peart
The Revelation of Jesus Christ, by Donald Peart
Jude—Translation and Commentary, by Donald Peart
Obtaining the Better Resurrection, by Donald Peart
Manifestations from Our Lord Jesus ...by Donald and Judith Peart).
Obtaining the Better Resurrection, by Donald Peart
The New Testament, Dr. Donald Peart Exegesis
The Tree of Life, By Dr. Donald Peart
The Spirit and Power of John, the Baptist by Dr. Donald Peart
The Shattered and the Healing by Judith Peart
Is She Married to a Husband? by Donald Peart
The Ugliest Man God Made by Donald Peart
Does Answering the Call of God Impact Your Children? by Donald Peart
Victory Out-of-the Beast-the Harvest of the Earth by Donald Peart
The Order of Melchizedek by Donald Peart
Ezekiel-the House-the City-the Land (Interpreting the Patterns), by Donald Peart

Butter and Honey, Understanding how to Choose the Good and Refuse Evil, by Donald Peart

Contact Information:
Crown of Glory Ministries
P.O. Box 1041 Randallstown, MD 21133
donaldpeart7@gmail.com

www.ingramcontent.com/pod-product-compliance
Lightning Source LLC
Chambersburg PA
CBHW032145040426
42449CB00005B/412